15

of prayer with

BLESSED CHIARA BADANO

On a journey, it's good to have a guide. Even great saints took spiritual directors or confessors with them on their itineraries toward sanctity. Now you can be guided by the most influential spiritual figures of all time. The 15 Days of Prayer series introduces their deepest and most personal thoughts.

This popular series is perfect if you are looking for a gift, or if you want to be introduced to a particular guide and his or her spirituality. Each volume contains:

- ∞ A brief biography of the saint or spiritual leader
- ∞ A guide to creating a format for prayer or retreat
- ∞ Fifteen meditation sessions with focus points and reflection guides

15 days
of prayer with
BLESSED CHIARA BADANO

Florence Gillet

NEW CITY PRESS
Hyde Park, NY

Published in the United States by New City Press of the Focolare
202 Comforter Blvd., Hyde Park, NY 12538
www.newcitypress.com
©2015 Nouvelle Cité

Original title published in French
Prier 15 jours avec Chiara Luce
©2013 by Nouvelle Cité

Translated into Italian by Gloria Romagnoli
Pregare 15 giorni con Chiara Luce
©2013 Piero Gribaudi Editore srl

Translated from Italian edition by Bill Hartnett
Cover design by Durva Correia and Leandro de Leon

Library of Congress Cataloging-in-Publication Data

Gillet, Florence.
 [Prier 15 jours avec Chiara Luce. English]
 15 days of prayer with Blessed Chiara Badano / by Florence Gillet.
 pages cm
 "Original title published in French, Prier 15 jours avec Chiara Luce
©2013 by Nouvelle Cité, then translated into the Italian edition, Pregare
15 giorni con CHIARA LUCE 2013 Piero Gribaudi Editore srl, translated
from the Italian edition by Bill Hartnett."
 Summary: "Throughout her young life Chiara Luce united herself
closely to Christ. Her faith shines through. Retracing her human and
spiritual journey before the illness, we then learn of her ecclesial and
communitarian side, which are a necessary corollary of her union with
the Crucified-Risen Lord"-- Provided by publisher.
 ISBN 978-1-56548-554-9 (alk. paper)
 1. Luce, Chiara, 1971-1990. 2. Catholics--Italy--Biography. 3. Spiritual
life--Catholic Church. 4. Prayer--Catholic Church. I. Hartnett, Bill,
translator. II. Title. III. Title: Fifteen days of prayer with Blessed Chiara
Badano.
 BX4705.L795535G5513 2015
 269'.6--dc23
 2015005147

Printed in the United States of America

Contents

How to Use
This Book

*A*n old Chinese proverb, or at least what I am able to recall of what is supposed to be an old Chinese proverb, goes something like this: "Even a journey of a thousand miles begins with a single step." When you think about it, the truth of the proverb is obvious. It is impossible to begin any project, let alone a journey, without taking the first step. I think it might also be true, although I cannot recall if another Chinese proverb says it, "that the first step is often the hardest." Or, as someone else once observed, "the distance between a thought and the corresponding action needed to implement the idea takes the most energy." I don't know who shared that perception with me but I am certain it was not an old Chinese master!

With this ancient proverbial wisdom, and the not-so-ancient wisdom of an unknown contemporary sage still fresh, we move from proverbs to presumptions. How do these relate to the task before us?

I am presuming that if you are reading this introduction it is because you are contemplating a journey. My presumption is that you are preparing for a spiritual journey and that you have taken at least some of the first steps necessary to prepare for this journey. I also presume, and please excuse me if I am making too many presumptions, that in your preparation for the spiritual journey you have determined that you need a guide. From deep within the recesses of your deepest self, there was something that called you to consider Dorothy Day as a potential companion. If my presumptions are correct, may I congratulate you on this decision? I think you have made a wise choice, a choice that can be confirmed by yet another source of wisdom, the wisdom that comes from practical experience.

Even an informal poll of experienced travelers will reveal a common opinion; it is very difficult to travel alone. Some might observe that it is even foolish. Still others may be even stronger in their opinion and go so far as to insist that it is necessary to have a guide, especially when you are traveling into uncharted waters and into territory that you have not yet experienced. I am of the personal opinion that a traveling companion is welcome under all circumstances. The thought of traveling alone, to some exciting destination without someone to share the journey with does not capture my imagination or channel my enthusiasm. However, with that being noted, what is simply a matter of preference on the normal journey becomes a matter of necessity when a person embarks on a spiritual journey.

The spiritual journey, which can be the most challenging of all journeys, is experienced best with a guide, a companion, or at the very least, a friend in whom you have placed your trust. This observation is not a preference or an opinion but rather an established spiritual necessity. All of the great saints with whom I am familiar had a spiritual director or a confessor who journeyed with them. Admittedly, at times the saints might well have traveled far beyond the experience of their guide and companion but more often than not they would return to their director and reflect on their experience. Understood in this sense, the director and companion provided a valuable contribution and necessary resource. When I was learning how to pray (a necessity for anyone who desires to be a full-time and public "religious person"), the community of men that I belonged to gave me a great gift. Between my second and third year in college, I was given a one-year sabbatical, with all expenses paid and all of my personal needs met. This period of time was called novitiate. I was officially designated as a novice, a beginner in the spiritual journey, and I was assigned a "master," a person who was willing to lead me. In addition to the master, I was provided with every imaginable book and any other resource that I could possibly need. Even with all that I was provided, I did not learn how to pray because of the books and the unlimited resources, rather it was the master, the companion who was the key to the experience.

One day, after about three months of reading, of quiet and solitude, and of practicing all of the methods and descriptions of prayer that were available to me, the master called. "Put away the books, forget the method, and just listen." We went into a room, became quiet, and tried to recall the presence of God, and then, the master simply prayed out loud and permitted me to listen to his prayer. As he prayed, he revealed his hopes, his dreams, his struggles, his successes, and most of all, his relationship with God. I discovered as I listened that his prayer was deeply intimate but most of all it was self-revealing. As I learned about him, I was led through his life experience to the place where God dwells. At that moment I was able to understand a little bit about what I was supposed to do if I really wanted to pray.

The dynamic of what happened when the master called, invited me to listen, and then revealed his innermost self to me as he communicated with God in prayer, was important. It wasn't so much that the master was trying to reveal to me what needed to be said; he was not inviting me to pray with the same words that he used, but rather that he was trying to bring me to that place within myself where prayer becomes possible. That place, a place of intimacy and of self-awareness, was a necessary stop on the journey and it was a place that I needed to be led to. I could not have easily discovered it on my own.

The purpose of the volume that you hold in your hand is to lead you, over a period of fifteen days or, maybe more realistically, fifteen prayer periods, to a place where prayer is possible. If you already have a regular experience and practice of prayer, perhaps this volume can help lead you to a deeper place, a more intimate relationship with the Lord.

It is important to note that the purpose of this book is not to lead you to a better relationship with Dorothy Day, your spiritual companion. Although your companion will invite you to share some of his deepest and most intimate thoughts, your companion is doing so only to bring you to that place where God dwells. After all, the true measurement of all companions for the journey is that they bring you to the place where you need to be, and then they step back, out of the picture. A guide who brings you to the desired destination and then sticks around is a very unwelcome guest!

Many times I have found myself attracted to a particular idea or method for accomplishing a task, only to discover that what seemed to be inviting and helpful possessed too many details. All of my energy went to the mastery of the details and I soon lost my enthusiasm. In each instance, the book that seemed so promising ended up on my bookshelf, gathering dust. I can assure you, it is not our intention that this book end up in your bookcase, filled with promise, but unable to deliver.

There are three simple rules that need to be followed in order to use this book with a measure of satisfaction.

Place: It is important that you choose a place for reading that provides the necessary atmosphere for reflection and that does not allow for too many distractions. Whatever place you choose needs to be comfortable, have the necessary lighting, and finally, have a sense of "welcoming" about it. You need to be able to look forward to the experience of the journey. Don't travel steerage if you know you will be more comfortable in first class and if the choice is realistic for you. On the other hand, if first class is a distraction and you feel more comfortable and more yourself in steerage, then it is in steerage that you belong.

My favorite place is an overstuffed and comfortable chair in my bedroom. There is a light over my shoulder, and the chair reclines if I feel a need to recline. Once in a while, I get lucky and the sun comes through my window and bathes the entire room in light. I have other options and other places that are available to me but this is the place that I prefer.

Time: Choose a time during the day when you are most alert and when you are most receptive to reflection, meditation, and prayer. The time that you choose is an essential component. If you are a morning person, for example, you should choose a time that is in the morning. If you are more alert in the afternoon, choose an afternoon time slot; and if evening is your preference, then by all means choose the evening. Try to avoid "peak" periods in your daily routine when you know that you might be disturbed. The time that you choose needs to be your time and needs to work for you.

It is also important that you choose how much time you will spend with your companion each day. For some it will be possible to set aside enough time in order to read and reflect on all the material that is offered for a given day. For others, it might not be possible to devote one time to the suggested material for the day, so the prayer period may need to be extended for two, three, or even more sessions. It is not important how long it takes you; it is only important that it works for you and that you remain committed to that which is possible.

For myself I have found that fifteen minutes in the early morning, while I am still in my robe and pajamas and before my morning coffee, and even before I prepare myself for the day, is the best time. No one expects to see me or to interact with me because I have not yet "announced" the fact that I am awake or even on the move. However, once someone hears me in the bathroom, then my window of opportunity is gone. It is therefore important to me that I use the time that I have identified when it is available to me.

Freedom: It may seem strange to suggest that freedom is the third necessary ingredient, but I have discovered that it is most important. By freedom I understand a certain "stance toward life," a "permission to be myself and to be gentle and understanding of who I am." I am constantly amazed at how the human person so easily sets himself or herself up for disappointment and perceived failure. We so easily make judgments about ourselves and our actions and our choices, and very often those judgments are negative, and not at all helpful.

For instance, what does it really matter if I have chosen a place and a time, and I have missed both the place and the time for three days in a row? What does it matter if I have chosen, in that twilight time before I am completely awake and still a little sleepy, to roll over and to sleep for fifteen minutes more? Does it mean that I am not serious about the journey, that I really don't want to pray, that I am just fooling myself when I say that my prayer time is important to me? Perhaps, but I prefer to believe that it simply means that I am tired and I just wanted a little more sleep. It doesn't mean anything more than that. However, if I make it mean more than that, then I can become discouraged, frustrated, and put myself into a state where I might more easily give up. "What's the use? I might as well forget all about it."

The same sense of freedom applies to the reading and the praying of this text. If I do not find the introduction to each day helpful, I don't need to read it. If I find the questions for reflection at the end of the appointed day repetitive, then I should choose to close the book and go my own way. Even if I discover that the reflection offered for the day is not the one that I prefer and that the one for the next day seems more inviting, then by all means, go on to the one for the next day.

That's it! If you apply these simple rules to your journey you should receive the maximum benefit and you will soon find yourself at your destination. But be prepared to be surprised. If you have never been on a spiritual journey you should know that the "travel brochures" and the other descriptions that you might have heard are nothing compared to the real thing. There is so much more than you can imagine.

A final prayer of blessing suggests itself:

Lord, catch me off guard today. Surprise me
with some moment of
 beauty or pain
So that at least for the moment
I may be startled into seeing that you
   are here in all your splendor,
Always and everywhere,
Barely hidden,
Beneath,
Beyond,
Within this life I breathe.

Frederick Buechner

Rev. Thomas M. Santa, CSsR
Liguori, Missouri

A Brief Biography

*C*hiara Luce Badano was born on October 29, 1971, in Sassello, Italy, a small village in Piedmont, just north of the Ligurian Apennines. She was the only child of a couple who had waited eleven years for her birth.

The village where she was born, which has less than 2,000 residents, is a popular resort for the city-dwellers of neighboring Savona and Genoa because of its natural beauty and pleasant climate. As a child little Chiara was much loved by her extended family—her grandparents, aunts, and uncles—and she was very happy growing up there, which she fondly called her "little Switzerland." Sassello is also famous throughout Italy for its *amaretti* cookies and for its porcini mushrooms, which Chiara and her family collected every August.

Her parents—her truck-driver father and housewife mother—surrounded their long-awaited child with tenderness and affection.

Her upbringing, without being rigid, was by no means permissive. Her mother, especially, educated her in the Catholic faith. Like all children she had her ups and downs, sad and happy moments, and at times was even a bit rebellious. She gladdened everyone's life with her pleasant, open, and generous personality.

When she was four years old, she gave away her favorite toys to poor children. When she was five, she learned of children dying of hunger in Africa and decided to help them.

An important event in her life took place in 1980 when, through a woman in town, she came to know about the Focolare, an ecclesial movement begun in 1943 by Chiara Lubich (1920-2008). The Focolare spread rapidly throughout Italy and Europe and, in the late 1950s, to North and South America. It proposed placing God in the center of one's life, putting the gospel—particularly the new commandment of mutual love—into practice through concrete actions, and living so that "all may be one."*

She became friends with Chicca Coriasco, a teenager not much older than herself, who was already involved in the Movement. Their relationship, based on their commitment to live together for Jesus, was a milestone in Chiara

---

* See Jn 17:21.

Badano's life. She already knew the gospels, since her parish priest had given her a copy for her first Holy Communion (May 27, 1979), and because her mother told her the stories and parables of Jesus along with bedtime stories and fables. Through her relationship with Chicca, Chiara Badano passed from fairy tales to an actual person who was both real and near: Jesus.

From then on, she became involved and took part in regular Focolare gatherings for children between 9 and 17 years of age, called "Gen 3" (the third generation of people involved in the Focolare)*. In May 1981, a large event for families of the Focolare Movement was held at the Sport Palace of Rome. Chiara Badano attended with her parents, Ruggero and Maria Teresa. Shortly thereafter, her mother and father also became involved in the movement.

That summer, by herself, she attended the "Mariapolis," a summer gathering of several days open to anyone, where gospel life is deepened. It includes programs designed for different age groups, and she joined with young people her age.

---

* The Gen 3 are boys and girls, aged 9 to 17, who commit themselves to living the gospel in their daily life. They meet together to share their experiences of life, and they also promote projects to involve other children in activities to benefit those in need or to spread the culture of unity.

During that Mariapolis, Chiara heard of Lubich's challenge to the Gen 3. She called for them to be a generation of saints, "to build a new world...it's not enough to have technicians, scientists and politicians. We need people who are wise—we need saints."[1] Chiara made her decision. Another topic discussed was Christ crucified, especially the moment of his forsakenness, the culmination of his suffering. Indeed, Chiara Lubich never hesitated to present, even to children, what lies at the heart of Christian life: the crucified-risen Christ, to whom we express our love by embracing him in the sufferings of daily life. With the freshness of a nine-year-old, Chiara Badano began to experience—as she says in her own words—that *"in retrospect, overcoming pain makes you free."* In June 1983, she told Chiara Lubich about her decision to consider Jesus forsaken *"[her] first spouse."*

This was the beginning of a personal correspondence with Chiara Lubich, whom she considered her spiritual mother. In her letters, she addressed Lubich as "Mamma." When she was eleven years old, she wrote:

> Chiara, I can't find the words to thank you, but I just know that I owe everything to you and to God.

Her adolescence was characterized by friendships, sports, reading, and taking part in Focolare events. At first there were only two girls at the meetings: Chiara and Chicca Coriasco, who in the end became like a sister to her. But soon other girls joined in.

Their point of reference was the Focolare house in Genoa, where occasional meetings were held for the Gen 3 of the whole area. One of the women from that house, the assistant to the Gen 3, would provide formation materials, but mostly she kept up a personal relationship with each of the girls. Chiara opened herself to the Gen assistant, sharing her small trials and temptations, but also her acts of love for Jesus forsaken.

From 1982 to 1985 she attended middle school, earning on her report card a mark of "good," the middle of the Italian grading scale at that time. She then enrolled at a liberal arts high school in Savona, about an hour away. To make it easier for her to attend school, her family moved there. Leaving her "little Switzerland" was very difficult for her, but out of love for Jesus forsaken she consented to the move.

She had a hard first year in high school, most likely because of a personality conflict with a particular teacher, and was required to repeat the year. She started second year in September 1987, but she didn't do very well and had to attend summer school in 1988 to bring up her grades.

A few days before her seventeenth birth-day, just after she had begun her third year of high school, something unexpected happened. During a tennis match she felt a sharp pain in her shoulder. The doctors, thinking it to be nothing more than a torn muscle, were not worried. In early February of 1989, however, she received the alarming diagnosis: osteosar-coma, one of the most aggressive forms of bone cancer.

She immediately underwent surgery in Turin, and then returned home, not yet fully aware of the seriousness of her illness. On March 14, however, when she began chemo-therapy at the oncology unit, the shock sank in.

On that day, completely aware of what she was doing, she said "yes" to Jesus forsaken, a "yes" she would repeat again and again with each new surprise from the illness, a "yes" that would punctuate the final days of her journey on earth. Not only did she accept the will of God, she desired it. That would be her mantra, the theme that ran through the long months of illness and intense pain:

If you want it, Jesus, then I want it too.

In May she lost the use of her legs. On June 5th she had to undergo another surgery, this time on her spine. On July 19 an internal hem-orrhage led her doctors to presume that she was nearing the end of her life. But then, for a few months, the tumor seemed to shrink, giving her a period of remission.

On October 29, her eighteenth birthday, her parents and friends were all together to celebrate with her. Two months later, on Christmas Eve, she had a relapse and had to be readmitted to the hospital. Spending Christmas there took her by surprise, but Chiara recommitted herself and "tried to love Jesus," as she said with great simplicity to the Archbishop of Turin when he visited her and remarked about the peace shining on her face.

On December 30, Chiara Lubich replied to a letter Chiara Badano had written her, offering a sentence from the Gospel of John that could be a watchword for her life: *"Those who abide in me and I in them bear much fruit, because apart from me you can do nothing"* (Jn 15:5). She wrote back, *"I feel like it's really for me!"*

On January 24, 1990, she underwent emergency surgery, but it did not help her condition. In the months that followed, the pain in her legs increased, and in June she returned home where she remained for the rest of her journey.

On July 26, Chiara Lubich gave her a new name, "Luce."*

---

* Focolare members sometimes asked Chiara Lubich for a new name that would help them on their journey to holiness. Chiara Badano's new name, "Luce," means "Light."

There was a constant coming and going of visitors. People gathered around her bed, or outside in the courtyard trying to make themselves useful, asking for news about her condition, bringing her small presents and offering support to her parents. All of them went away with an unusual sense of happiness: *"We didn't know who the patient was, us or her,"* said many visitors to the Badano home.[*]

During those two years of suffering Chiara Luce Badano was supported by the bishop, her parish priests, members of the Focolare Movement, and especially her parents. Together they did their best to embrace every opportunity to love, to be rooted in love in the present moment. As each day passed, Chiara Luce's love for Jesus became more and more refined. She offered up her suffering, refusing morphine because it *"takes away my clarity."* She wanted nothing *"but [her] sufferings to offer Jesus."* Everything around her spoke of life and eternity. As she felt death approaching, she prepared her funeral, down to the most minute details. She came to consider death as the consummation of her marriage with her Spouse, and so she asked to be dressed in a white wedding gown, which, she said, should be very simple. A friend of the family made the gown,

---

[*] Summ, 48.

and her inseparable friend, Chicca, helped her try it on. She and Chicca also chose the songs for the funeral and rehearsed them together. Her final words, whispered in her mother's ear, were:

Be happy, because I am.

She died at dawn on October 7, 1990.

Over 2,000 people attended her funeral Mass, celebrated by Bishop Livio Maritano. After her death her reputation for holiness began to spread. Many wanted to follow her luminous example, and felt she had helped them grow in their faith. Her story soon became known beyond Italy and Europe into Africa, where several clinics were named after her.

On June 11, 1999, at the request of the local bishop, the diocesan investigation leading to the beatification process began. It was completed two years later, after the testimony of seventy-two witnesses. On July 3, 2008, Benedict XVI recognized her heroic virtue and declared her "venerable." On December 19, 2009, the decree approving a miracle attributed to her interces-sion opened the way to her beatification, which was celebrated on September 25, 2010, at the Marian shrine of Our Lady of the Divine Love, near Rome. Over 12,000 attended, most of them young people.

Introduction

*O*ver the course of the months in which I studied the life of Chiara Luce Badano and wrote this book, I have come to realize that this very young woman—a person of our own times, who didn't have any special form of consecration in the church other than baptism (the so-called "royal priesthood")—bore witness above all to the beauty of being a disciple of Christ. As such, she kept herself in an attitude of listening, trusting and conforming herself to Jesus the Teacher to the point of becoming similar to him. Through Chiara Luce Badano, God offers us the gift of a reminder that people are still being called today to reproduce the image of Christ and to become sons and daughters in the Son.

Throughout her entire life, particularly during the two years of her illness, Chiara Luce united herself closely to Christ. She lived the Christian vocation in an exemplary fashion, imitating the sentiments of Jesus.* Through her extraordinary experience, Chiara Luce has something to tell us and, as a daughter in the Son, her word is credible and we should listen to it.

Chiara Luce grew within a particular context, that of the Focolare Movement, which proposed a way of life that she embraced wholeheartedly. In order to grasp the content and scope of her words and actions, it will be necessary at times to situate them within the spirituality of the Focolare so as to highlight what lies at the root of her message.

On the other hand, her life was fashioned by the Word of God, which she echoed in a splendid way. One of the main features of these commentaries will be to highlight this constant reference to the Word, in order to embrace, above and beyond Chiara Luce but thanks to her, the presence of God in his Word.

By allowing herself to be transformed in Jesus, she gained a privileged knowledge of him, a clear and living faith that puzzled many of those who came to know her. Some of the commentary below underlines certain aspects of her faith, with the help of the Creed. In other parts, we will examine her attitude toward the

* See Phil 2:5.

mysteries of the faith, her "believing," and also her clear "knowledge" of the faith.

Since Christ's resurrection is the core of the Christian faith, Chiara Luce can be considered above all as a witness that he is truly risen because she herself lived as someone who was "risen in Christ,"* particularly during the final months of her life on earth. In the fifteen days of prayer contained in this book, the first seven, which describe her human and spiritual journey before the illness, provide a key to her spiritual life. Her faith shines through in days eight through eleven. The final sections, days twelve to fifteen, present another dimension of her spiritual life, the ecclesial and communitarian, which are a necessary corollary of her union with the Crucified-Risen Lord.

This book, published not by chance at the close of a year that the Church dedicated to faith, will show us how Chiara Luce reached the point of having such a vibrant, living faith and what path she followed to achieve it.

May she accompany us for these fifteen days, helping us to grow in love and in faith, and to taste the unspeakable joy of being among those for whom faith is not in vain, for they are the witnesses that He is truly risen.

_____

* See Eph 2:6.

Day One

Jesus, the Travelling Companion

When Mamma left she seemed a bit worried and said: "Chiara, you're on your own now, so try to behave yourself!" But I told her, "Mamma, I'm not on my own. Jesus is here."[2]

"I chose Him."[3]

*T*hese two simple and seemingly unpretentious statements introduce us into these fifteen days of meditation and prayer.

They were uttered at a particular moment, when Chiara Luce's mother, Maria Teresa, was saying goodbye to her nine-year-old daughter as she left for her first Focolare meeting. The simplicity of her words provides a key to the spiritual figure of Chiara Luce.

The presence of Jesus, the assurance that he is there, the fervent desire to do everything in her power so that he would be there, remained with Chiara Luce throughout her life. Being-in-relation with him was her strength, but even more it was her innermost self. At eleven or twelve years of age she wrote:

> Besides the powerful joy of belonging to the Gen unit,[*] I felt Jesus near to me.[4]

To her friends she had to admit:

> You can never even imagine what my relationship with Jesus is like now.[5]

In her final hours she wrote,

> If the devil comes, I'm not afraid of him anymore, because Jesus is stronger.[6]

She welcomed the gift of Jesus' presence and responded with a commitment to be with him, a decision she never turned back on, not even in the face of difficulty, as when she had to repeat a year of school or had to move from the Gen 3 group for adolescents to the Gen 2 group

---

[*] Gen unit. A small group of boys or girls who are committed to living the spirituality of unity of the Focolare together.

for older teenagers. She did not turn back even when she was informed of her terminal illness.

These words actually are strong enough to make us reflect and even transform us. The first are deeply rooted in Scripture. *"I will be with you." "Do not be afraid."* There are numerous examples in both the Old and New Testament of God "being with" the ones he has chosen. At times these words express God's commitment in view of some mission: *"I shall be with you,"* the Lord says to Moses (Ex 3:12). At times there is a condition attached, such as obeying the commandments: *"If you will listen to all that I command you, walk in my ways, and do what is right in my sight by keeping my statutes and my commandments, as David my servant did, I will be with you, and will build you an enduring house, as I built for David, and I will give Israel to you"* (1 Kings 11:38).

The presence of God carries with it the certainty of being able to overcome obstacles: *"And I will make you to this people a fortified wall of bronze; they will fight against you,* but they shall not prevail over you, *for I am with you to save you and deliver you, says the Lord"* (Jer 15:20). Since God commits himself to stand beside his elect, he requires trust from them. The promise of the divine presence is usually accompanied by the injunction "do not be afraid."

The extraordinary reality of God's presence among humankind is fully revealed in the
New Testament, which conveys the unconditional *Good News of Jesus Christ.* The Gospel of
Mathew in particular is structured around the
promise of "God-among-us." It begins with the
name to be given to the child, *Emmanuel,* "God
with us,"* and ends with the promise of Jesus'
presence for all days until the end of the world.†
The opening and the closing of Matthew's
Gospel convey the essence of the Good News:
the presence of the "God-among-us." The community is built upon this presence and in it. To
say that Jesus is Emmanuel, the God who lives
among us and will always be with us until the
end of the world, is another way of saying that
he is alive in the church and in the world, that
he is risen.

Chiara Luce had a profound sense of the
presence of the Risen Lord who lived in her
and in whom she wished to live. In this, she
leads us along a path of true prayer. We recall
the woman with the hemorrhage, who was certain of being healed if only she could touch the
hem of Jesus' garment.‡ She managed to reach
him, and, just as everyone was pushing in

---

* See Mt 1:21; 23.
† See Mt 28:20.
‡ See Lk 8: 42-48.

around him, Jesus felt "touched" by only one person. To the great surprise of the disciples, as Jesus was being pushed from all sides, he asks, "Who touched me?" (Lk 8:45). In other words, the real contact took place only for this woman who had faith.

Commenting on this passage, Pasquale Foresi wrote: "Many had 'prayed' Him, but only one found the way to speak to him. She had found 'prayer,' and Jesus felt that a power had been released from him because of that humble, silent, faith-filled prayer of abandonment."[7] Is that not true prayer: contact with the Beloved and mutual love?

This brings us back to Chiara Badano's decision to be with Jesus, and it is a major feature of her personality. It can be useful in understanding the full scope of her decision, to know that Chiara Lubich, precisely during that period when Chiara began to go to the Focolare, proposed holiness, to all the members of the movement. She explained the requirements to do so, the great and small sacrifices. Toward autumn 1981 she proposed a "holy journey," a term suggested by a psalm that calls blessed the one "in whose heart are the highways to Zion" (Ps 84:5). One must make a decision, fully aware of the cause, a decision to "be with Jesus."

"I chose Him." Chiara Luce had taken up this "holy journey" in total freedom. She

had pointed herself toward Someone, toward
Another outside of herself. Her decision has
a sense of "forever," because this journey will
take her to the end of her life. Her "yes" is an
effort that takes place within time, within the
time of the journey.

I believe in one Lord Jesus Christ, the Only Begotten Son of God

Chiara Luce's decision was rooted in an attitude of faith: she entrusted herself to the One
who "is with her" and had given her, throughout her life and death, undeniable proof of his
love. Her "travelling companion" is an expert,
and she, who had handed him the roadmap,
never snatched it back from his hands. In fact,
this "believing" was a matter of trust. The gospel offers an example of this in the centurion
whose servant is paralyzed. The centurion
entrusts himself completely to Jesus, who has
greater authority than he does: *"Lord, I am not
worthy that you should come under my roof, but only
say the word and my servant will be healed."**

This passage from Matthew shows how
easily Jesus is moved by trust. Amazed, he
declares that anyone with such faith will one
day sit at table with Abraham, Isaac and Jacob

---

* See Mt 8:8.

in the kingdom of heaven.* And isn't inviting us to sit at table in the kingdom another way of saying "You will be with me"?

---

* See Mt 8:10.

Day Two

It Was Jesus Who Asked You

*I thought: "I'm accompanying Jesus, who has abandoned himself to my shoulders."…
What I would have lost if you hadn't insisted that I stay alone with Grandpa(!)
and I thank you.*[8]

We have simple but profound examples of Chiara Luce's love for Jesus in the poor and ailing, like the one cited above. On August 15, 1987, her parents had asked her to stay with her maternal grandfather. He was ill, but there was no indication he would die that very night.

Her father recounts:

In that moment Chiara feared she wouldn't be able to stay with him in his need, but she agreed. When my wife and I returned, the joy was shining in her eyes. She told us that she had to accompany her grandfather to the bathroom, that she had managed to do it and, as he leaned on her, she thought: *"I'm accompanying Jesus who has abandoned himself to my shoulders."*[9]

Her mother, however, recalled Chiara saying this of the moment:

When my grandfather put his arms around my neck, I felt the embrace of Jesus.[10]

Her mother mentioned another incident:

One day during the six o'clock evening Mass, [a rather strange young man whom people avoided] sat in the pew in front of me. He turned to me and asked me to sit next to him. I told him no.... Then I felt remorse [and I moved into the pew with him]. When I returned home, I told my daughter about the incident. She turned serious, looked me in the eyes and asked: *"You did that?"* Then she told me the reason for her disappointment: *"Jesus was in him!"* I replied: "You're right," so then I went to sit with him....And Chiara said, *"Thank goodness!"*[11]

As she was beginning her holy journey, Chiara Luce understood Christianity to be, above all, concrete love that is translated into concrete service toward one's neighbor. She was deeply struck by a sentence from the story of the final judgment in the Gospel of Matthew, which is so basic in Focolare spirituality. "I was hungry and you gave me to eat." And the surprise: "But when did we see you hungry and give you to eat?" For Chiara Luce, being able to find the Lord in a poor person, whether old or strange or addicted to drugs, was finding today's "least." [12] It was an opportunity, a "good deal," a wonderful opportunity for expressing her love to Jesus.

The topic of love of neighbor was presented and discussed extensively during the gatherings for children and young teens that Chiara Badano attended. These concepts were the annual theme that Chiara Lubich offered to the entire movement that year:

> "We are the ones who need *them* in order to possess eternal life....Love for the poor becomes a source of great peace and hope when we realize that, since Jesus considers as done to him whatever we do for those in need, he becomes indebted to us and we become his creditors." [13]

For a small child like Chiara Luce, living
the Christian life in this way could have a play-
ful dimension. Isn't it a game, a most exciting
game, to be with Jesus, becoming completely
involved with him, concretely, by loving a poor
person, perceiving his response and his almost
grateful acknowledgement in an exchange of
love?

A serious game, nevertheless, that puts a
mirror in front of the quality of our faith. While
Chiara Luce was eager, I would say, to demon-
strate her love for Jesus in the poor, she did so
because she was basing herself on his word and
obeying it. "At your word," I will love this poor
person, perhaps without understanding why or
how you are present, but I trust in you, with no
ifs, ands, or buts. A bit like Peter, after fishing
the whole night and not catching a single fish.
He obeyed an irrational order: *"If you say so, I
will let down the nets."* * Instant adherence is a
particular characteristic of children, and aren't
we all called to convert and become children?†

---

* See Lk 5:5.
† See Mt 18:3.

I believe in Jesus Christ who by the Holy Spirit was incarnate of the Virgin Mary

As presented in the New Testament and as Chiara Luce lived it, faith is primarily "listening" and "obedience."* This is illustrated in the story in John of the man born blind.† Earlier, just before meeting the blind man, Jesus had declared: *"I am the light of the world. When he had said this, he spit on the ground, made mud with the saliva, and spread the mud on the man's eyes, saying to him: 'Go, wash in the pool of Siloam' (which means Sent). Then he went and washed and came back able to see"* (Jn 9:6-7). The first stage of the blind man's "believing" is obedience to an order: Go and wash. It will be followed by other stages: recognizing Jesus as a prophet (v.17); openly declaring that the one who cured him cannot be a sinner (v.31); or, better, that the one who cured him could only come from God (v.33).

Let us begin with the first stage, that of obeying an order. With her faith and obedience to Jesus' words ("you did it to me"), Chiara Luce received a light that was not of this world: *"What I would have lost if you had not insisted* [that is, if I had not listened to you]?" What was she

---

referring to? Most likely she was referring to the
presence of God that satisfied her completely.
Perhaps she had perceived in a more evident
way the infinite and irrevocable love of God
for every person, destined to be another Christ.

By believing, we accomplish a kind of exodus out of ourselves. We trust in the word that
requires us to move out from our own self-
centeredness and we experience that God is
totally "other." In our own little way, we relive
Abraham's faith and obedience regarding
where he would spend his life: *"Go from your
country and your kindred and your father's house"**
and Mary's faith and obedience regarding her
plans in life: *"You will conceive in your womb and
bear a son."†* These are our parents in the faith.

Let us highlight once again that Jesus
himself accomplishes an exodus by becoming
present in the sick, the prisoner and the hungry. He indicates that they are "him," another
him. The very essence of the incarnation is
expressed in this exodus of Jesus: God truly
became man like us; he placed himself in our
hands and united himself to every creature—
the humblest, the poorest, the most scorned.
Each and every person, each and every life has
a link with him, especially the person who for
any reason suffers.

---

* Gen 12:1
† Lk 1:31

Being referred to another outside our self disorients us. But Chiara Luce's experience shows that we are redirected toward the one true God through the one whom he has sent, Jesus Christ. This is faith: allowing ourselves to be disoriented for a moment in order to set out in the right direction.

Day Three

I've Found Friends That Are Different from the Others

The girls I met were good and kind, different from the ones at school. And we tried to help each other to live for Jesus.[14]

[Dear Orietta, Dear Luca] Only now at this moment [of your departure] have I understood what a deep bond of unity unites us! Knowing that you were already in the back yard was very important for me. Thinking back to that summer I felt a great joy in my heart and a spontaneous thought comes to me: "Thank you, Jesus, for these relationships that are so 'beautiful' with these two [sister and brother]!"[15]

*[Dear Chicca] I always feel you very near.
Let's begin a new year plunging ourselves
into the Holy Journey. I love you. Let's
always keep Jesus in our midst.*"[16]

*T*he tone and style of these three texts,
taken from letters and postcards, might
seem dissimilar and unconnected. Yet they
have one thing in common: Jesus. Moreover,
all three highlight a particular type of interpersonal relationship in him. Truly, Chiara Luce
was completely fascinated by one relationship
in particular, the one between her and the
other children in the Focolare, a relationship
that was substantially different from the friendships she had been accustomed to with others.

These three texts, each in its own way,
reveal a quality of friendship and relationship
that surprises and fascinates Chiara Luce. She
experiences the joy of reciprocity, the fruit of
Jesus' new commandment, one that cannot
be lived alone: *"Just as I have loved you, you also
should love one another"* (Jn 13:34). When this
commandment is put into practice, you can tell
neither where love begins nor where it ends.
Time and time again, you love and let yourself
be loved. It is a collective love, circular, as is
the unity it evokes:

You feel it, you enjoy it....Everyone enjoys its presence, everyone suffers its absence. It's peace, gladness, love, ardor, an atmosphere of highest generosity.[17]

This mutual love that leads to unity is concrete; it calls for an asceticism at which Chiara Luce was an expert, as seen in an episode recounted by a classmate. Fourteen or fifteen years old, they were invited to spend the last few days of summer at Chiara's house. One afternoon they could not go out. The friend reports:

Her patience had no limits. One afternoon the weather kept us from going outside. We decided to play Monopoly. After only two rounds I was already bored, [so Chiara] right away proposed another game—I think it was Chutes and Ladders. After a while I was bored again and we changed games again, and then again, and again—all because of me. I'd make her prepare everything and then I wouldn't want to play the game, but not once did she reproach me, not once, she just began again without ever growing tired of me. She just smiled at me the whole time, always loving me, never demanding anything from me.[18]

Jesus spells out the measure of mutual love: *"As I have loved you."* Living the new commandment requires being the first to love, to accept love in the way the other person expresses it, not in the way we would like it to be expressed. It means knowing how to say thank you: *"Thank you, Jesus, for this relationship that is so beautiful,"* she writes to Luca and Orietta, in a letter dated September 14, 1990. She is referring to the relationship with the young couple over the summer holidays they spent in Sassello, during what would be the last summer of her life. Orietta arrived at the same time every day, and she hardly ever went into Chiara's bedroom; she only wanted to show her love by being near to her even just being out in the backyard.

Their relationship was based on far more than mere human respect, and they did not hesitate to declare openly their desire to live out the commandment of mutual love. Indeed, this was done by a pact, both implicit and explicit, to love one another in Jesus. Orietta writes:

> We tried to help one another to live for Jesus....together plunging ourselves into the Holy Journey....Let's always keep Jesus in our midst.[19]

The unity established as the fruit of mutual love brings the very presence of Jesus, according to his promise, *"For where two or three are gathered in my name, I am there among them"* (Mt 18:20).

Chicca shared one episode with the Gen 3 assistant of Genoa in 1985 or 1986, which represents this mutual love that blossomed into Jesus in their midst. Chiara Luce and Chicca met for their regular meeting in the village of Albisola. In order not to waste time moving around, they decided to have their meeting in a chapel near the bus stop.

> As soon as we entered [the chapel] we were enveloped in a very profound atmosphere. It was a deep sense of the divine, and so we went to sit in the first pew and began to read the little book on the Trinity,* line by line, explaining it in our own words and thinking about what the words meant. It seemed to us that the Trinity was so near, the Father, the Son, and the Holy Spirit.[20]

By living Jesus' new commandment to love one another with her "new friends," Chiara Luce entered more deeply into the mystery of the communion of love that is in God, which we call "Trinity."

Loving one another is already a participation in the love that comes from God: *"Beloved,*

---

* A book series on the fundamentals of the faith for Gen 3.

let us love one another, because love is from God;
everyone who loves is born of God and knows God.
Whoever does not love does not know God, for God is
love" (1 Jn 4:7-8). Loving one another increases
our understanding of this mystery. We know
the Father better, that he is Love who freely
gives, Love who from all eternity is the first to
love and is also called "the Beloved." We know
the Son better, the one who allows himself to
be loved, who eternally receives the Father's
love and loves the Father. We know the Spirit
who unites the Lover and the Beloved, and
who is also the ecstasy of love.

From our own human experience we know
what it means to be "for" the other, "with"
the other. This is the hidden mystery of God:
each divine Person lives entirely "with," "for,"
"in" the other two, in what the Eastern Church
Fathers call the *perichoresis*. Each Person lives
"for" the other, outside of self. The gospel
shows us Jesus who is turned toward the Father
(Jn 1:2), for the Father, and in the Father: *"The*
Father and I are one" (Jn 10:30). *"Everything of*
mine is yours, and everything of yours is mine" (Jn
17:10). *"No one knows the Son except the Father,*
and no one knows the Father except the Son" (Mt
11:27). Precisely in mutual love do we enter
into the knowledge and into the presence of
God the Trinity.

The texts we read today portray a very young girl who lives the mystery of God in her interpersonal relationships. At times she takes the initiative in loving, at other times she allows herself to be loved, or feels the need to emphasize unity in love. She does this in such a way that the word "together" suddenly unleashes all of its depth and force. Through her life she confesses: *"I believe in God who is a communion of love."*

She shows us how we too can enter into the life of communion that is God.

Day Four

God Loves Me Immensely

And yet God loves me.[21]

A person, a woman with a very bright and beautiful smile, came up to me, took my hand and offered me words of encouragement....Reasoning about it, I thought: "That was a coincidence." But then I wondered, "So why did she arrive at that exact moment? Precisely in that situation and, above all, with that light that seemed, I would say without exaggeration, supernatural?"... Then I realized that if we were always in this disposition, ready for all such signs, then God would send them to us! I realized also how often God does pass by and we don't even realize it.[22]

*G*od is love. God, who *"loved me and gave himself for me"* (Gal 2:20), invites us to share in his life. This good news has been sung for twenty centuries. It is the font that will always satisfy our thirst, the stupendous gift that down through the ages has shaped saints. *"Love is not loved!"* is what St. Francis of Assisi and his early companions cried out to everyone. *"God loves you immensely"* are the words that marked the beginning of the Focolare in 1943, which quickly spread to all of Italy and then to the world. *"So we have known and believe the love that God has for us"* (1 Jn 4:16). This sentence, which Chiara Lubich wished to be written on their common tomb if she and her first companions died during the war, encapsulates their real identity. Chiara Luce was nourished by this faith in God's love, and it wasn't just a theory, but rather was based on the concrete experience of the early days of the Focolare.

As a matter of fact, God always manifests his love in the story of humanity, in the great history of salvation, from Adam to Jesus, and in the small influences of the Holy Spirit in human history. The story of God's interventions in the early days of the Focolare had been referred to, illustrated and even acted out for and by the children. God's promises emerge from this story—promises fulfilled promptly, beyond all expectations, concrete signs of divine love and Providence. These eloquent signs continue to be a permanent invitation to believe in God's love and to respond to it by loving.

In her own small way Chiara Luce wished to relive this loving exchange with God, striving to love Jesus in every neighbor, committing herself together with others to live Jesus' new commandment, to bring his ineffable presence among us and in us.

Feeling loved by God unleashes unknown energies within us: the strength of loving back as we have been loved. Everything about Chiara Luce revolves around loving and longing for love. There is no trace in her of fearing God's judgment, no trace of fearing hell—only the joy of being able to respond to God's love by loving.

Like all of us, her faith was put to the test. As a child and later as a young teenager, the small sufferings of life could have corroded her faith in God's love. Yet she continued to believe, because she had learned that Jesus manifests his love fully on the cross, a folly which, far from being a stumbling block, for her became a springboard.

"And yet God loves me." Chiara Luce found the strength to acknowledge this even after violent muscle spasms. It bears witness to her desire, with the full force of her intelligence,

"for reasons that reason doesn't know," to adhere to love because Jesus has assumed our sufferings out of love. The presence of suffering that presented itself in her flesh became for her the sign of God's love. Because even in the signs that might seem contrary to love, what could be called "anti-signs," Chiara Luce chose to believe that there lie hidden the *super love.*

In certain circumstances, faith like hers gives rise to an explosion of love for God, as when during an unannounced medical exam, despite her fear and anguish, she managed to have trust. In a recording from September 10, 1990 (partially transcribed in the introduction), she described a most luminous woman who came to offer her encouragement and then disappeared. Neither she nor her parents ever discovered who this woman was.

Such signs from heaven are given to corroborate our loving acceptance of the "anti-signs." They are an anticipation of the Easter Resurrection that Chiara Luce repeatedly accepted. She writes:

> I saw how, if we were always in this disposition, ready for everything, how many signs God would send to us! I saw also how often God passes by us and we don't even realize it.

That means being ready for anything, ready to welcome God's love in every circumstance, without exception. Chiara Luce therefore inserted herself into a dynamic relationship of reciprocal love with God: she handed herself over with an act of complete trust in his love, and He manifested signs of his love to her. She had an attitude of loving exchange, an alliance, an irreversible accord interwoven with God throughout her life.

The Father Almighty

Chiara Luce did not remain trapped within the question: if God is love, why is there suffering? How can a God who permits suffering be omnipotent? Do we want to project onto God the human inability to bridge the gap between love and omnipotence? Her faith helped her overcome this dilemma, to know the breadth, length, heights and depths of love.[*]

Chiara Luce believed that God's love had taken on every earthly suffering, so that we no longer encounter suffering, but the One who had assumed it. Would such faith provoke a passive, indifferent attitude in the face of worldly misfortune? No. She leaped into action when she heard about five-year-old children dying of hunger in Africa. She stood up and said, *"Now we have to think about them."*[23] And whenever she learned that others were suf-

---

[*] See Eph 3:18.

fering, whether morally or physically, she did everything in her power to alleviate their pain.

In her admirable loving exchange with God, she likely understood the omnipotence of God as an omnipotence of love. God had entrusted the world to human beings so that we might continue his creation, and he had delegated this responsibility to us so that his love might rule in the world. He loved us so much that he made us his allies, entrusting his work to us. In short, he believed in us. He had given us love so that we might spread it liberally everywhere in the world.

For Chiara Luce the real meaning of life lay in this loving exchange between a Father and his children. Shortly before dying she said,

> You need to have the courage to put aside ambitions and plans that destroy the real meaning of life, which is to believe in God's love and that's all.[24]

Our love story with the Father is fruitful. Chiara Luce knew this; she was so certain of the Father's love that she waited to discover the fruits of her faith in his love. She waited to know them, to accept them, and to say thank you for them.

Day 5

Attuned to God

I've understood the importance of "cutting" in order to be only in the will of God, then again what St. Thérèse used to say: that before dying by the sword, one must die by pinpricks. I see that it's the little things I don't do so well, or the little sufferings, the ones I allow to escape me. So now I want to continue loving all of them like pinpricks.[25]

*D*uring the first Focolare gatherings that Chiara Luce attended, a recurring theme was the will of God. Those girls, so rooted in their faith in God's love, rejoiced to discover God's personal love, God's marvelous plan for each one of them that would gradually unfold over time as they lived out what he willed for them in the present moment. A frequently used image, the sun and its rays, was an eloquent reminder for Chiara Luce that by following our particular ray, each of us draws closer to God, but also to one another.

At a Gen Convention held in Turin in January 1986, the young women listened to a recording from 1981 in which Chiara Lubich shared her experience of the "holy journey" and explained the necessary condition for taking up that journey: deciding to do not one's own will, but the will of God. Following the talk the Focolare teenagers were presented with several age-appropriate examples of friends of God who had tried to do God's will.

A recording made at that convention captured the voice of Chiara Luce sharing her decision to do and to be the will of God. She understood that in order to do the will of God, she had to "lose," a strong verb that implies "cutting." What did that word mean to her? It meant to cut with anything that was not God's will in the present moment, to be uncompromising with herself and to never step out of her ray, whatever the cost. Yet, she immediately added, the ray of God's will is love.

The will of God coincides perfectly with his love that embraces all of human history in one magnificent plan. This is evident in the gift he has given us in his Son, Jesus Christ, who came to transform into love whatever seems to be "non-love". Through him, everything now works toward the good for those who love God.* This is the plan of God: to make us sons and daughters in the Son, free with the freedom of God, creators with the Creator.

From another perspective, what God wants is our sanctification,† that is, for us to share in his life; he wants us to "be love" as he is Love. In his priestly prayer, Jesus "wills" that we share in his glory: *"Father, I desire that those also, whom you have given me, may be with me where I am, to see my glory, which you have given me because you loved me before the foundation of the world"* (Jn 17:24). Jesus, who had always been attentive to obeying the Father's will, in this moment made a strong request to the Father for us.

Chiara Luce understood that we can act according to this plan of love; we can correspond to it by loving others. She realized that we cannot waste even a tiny piece of this plan, which is fulfilled in the very smallest things. Nor should we impede its completion by doing our own will. The will of God and love coincide, and Chiara Luce understood something St. Thérèse of Lisieux said, and that Chiara Lubich cited in her talk on the "holy journey:" *"Before dying by the sword, let us die by pinpricks."*[26]

---

* See Rm 8:28.
† See 1 Thes 4:3.

Like Thérèse, Chiara Luce wanted to accept the daily martyrdom of love all the way down to the little things. And she lived out the "cutting" that comes from authentic love, never wishing to draw back from it but cooperating with the hidden design of a plan that she trusted because it was divine. Chiara Luce demonstrates how a person who does the will of God is not passive, but an active creator.

She strove always to abide in love but, like the rest of us, sometimes forgot. Then she would regain control of herself and begin again, without any delay. To help her in this she looked to Jesus' parable of the two sons. Both had been asked to help their father in the vineyard. One agreed to go, but never did what his father asked. The other said no, but repented and did what the father asked.* Chiara Luce was happy to be like the second son, to be recognized, as Jesus said, as his sister and mother: *"'Who is my mother, and who are my brothers?' And stretching out his hand toward his disciples, he said, 'Here are my mother and my brothers! For whoever does the will of my Father in heaven is my brother and sister and mother'"* (Mt 12:48-49).

She understood that we have only *now* to do the will of God. Rooting ourselves in the present moment we reconnect, reunite with

---

* See Mt 21:28-31.

our source, our being "in God," who is the
source of every life and every love. Then the
heart rests in God even amid suffering. In a
school essay from the autumn of 1989, shortly
before she died she writes:

> Often a person does not live her life
> because she is immersed in moments
> that don't exist: either remembering
> the past or mourning over it, or being
> projected into the future. In reality,
> the only time we possess is the pres-
> ent moment.... By living the present,
> a person feels liberated because she
> is no longer crushed by the anguish
> of her past or by the worry about her
> future.

And she adds:

> It requires a constant effort to remain
> in this attitude.[27]

The present moment. Her father Ruggero,
brokenhearted at seeing his daughter dying,
asked her the secret to her serenity. She
explained what she learned from being ill and
yet ignoring the outcome of her illness:

> Try to live the present moment. You
> have to chop it into little pieces, live
> every single minute. Live every min-
> ute in union with Jesus.

And she added:

> Then God helps you.[28]

If you live the will of God in the present moment, you are not the prisoner of your own failures or of your own sins. You know that you can always begin again. By placing yourself in the present you place yourself in God who is there waiting for you. This was a constant for Chiara Luce. She had bad mood moments, little outbursts of anger, but she placed herself again in God, never allowing herself to be crushed by a sense of guilt.

One day shortly before her death, while in great pain, she asked her mother to read something for meditation, indicating a particular passage. It was the transcription of a telephone conference call in which Chiara Lubich explained the importance of living in the present and the benefits that doing so would bring. Among other things she said: *"It's by living the present moment that crosses become bearable."*

Lubich also cited St. Paul of the Cross:

> How fortunate that soul who rests in God's bosom, without thinking of the future, but seeking only to live moment by moment in God, with no other concern than to accomplish well his will in every circumstance.[29]

This was something Chiara Luce wanted to hear again and again, because it was her secret way of "being in God."

Day Six

Give

During this convention I rediscovered the gospel under a new light. I understood that I was not an authentic Christian because I wasn't living it all the way. Now I want this magnificent book to be the only reason for my life. I neither can nor want to remain illiterate of such an extraordinary message. Just as it was easy for me to learn the alphabet, so it should be easy for me to learn to live the gospel. I rediscovered that sentence which says, "Give and it will be given to you." I need to learn to trust Jesus, to believe in his immense love.[30]

C hiara Luce was fourteen years old when she wrote this in a letter to Chiara Lubich. She correlates three different things:

the richness of the Word of God that is offered in the gospel, the act of "giving," and faith in Jesus. At that time in her life, the conversations presented to the Gen 3 that she would have heard were all based on the Word of God, illustrated by real life testimonies. Another topic discussed with the Gen 3 at that time was the communion of goods.

These few lines show that she had grasped the special link between "gospel," "faith" (as trust), and "gift." In fact, these three terms refer back to each other; they are mutually related.

By "gospel," Chiara Badano means to say the words and actions of Jesus as narrated in the four gospels; and she underscores the importance of living these words one at a time, just as you would learn the alphabet, in order to be "clothed" in them and, little by little, become similar to Jesus. From this extraordinary message, she recalls the need to "give," going against the current of the world which is usually focused only on "having."

For Chiara Luce "giving" is not a philosophy or an ethical principle but a person, Jesus, who asks this of her, and to whom she entrusts herself.

Before knowing the Focolare, Chiara Luce had already experienced the joy of giving. As a small child she considered giving away her best toys. It wasn't easy, but after a moment of reflection, she chose to do so. Later, while preparing for her first Holy Communion, she desired to offer acts of love to Jesus.[31]

During the Gen 3 convention of 1985, she realized that she had been living the gospel mandate to give rather amateurishly, and decided to make it part of her regular behavior. She shared her experiences of life with the others, not to call attention to herself, but to offer as a gift what God had given her in life. To the Gen 3 meetings she brought small amounts of money she had saved, or one of her belongings that might be taking the place of God in her life. She felt a responsibility toward the spiritual family to which she belonged and toward its economy.

When you are very sick, it is a struggle to maintain an attitude of giving, yet this is what produced a special light that seemed to radiate from her face.

Learning that her friend Gianfranco Piccardo was on his way to Africa, she didn't want to hold on to anything for herself. She gave away for his mission everything the others had been giving to her. To her mom she said:

> Take that envelope, because I want Gian to have it for the poor children of Africa.[32]

Maria Teresa responded: *You mean all of it?*

Yes.[33]

She also gave her failures, her sufferings and her joys.

I offer Thee my nothingness.[34]

She shared a personal letter written to Chiara Lubich with a member of the Focolare. But first she said:

> You know, the last time I wrote to Chiara [Lubich] I kept it all to myself, I didn't want anyone to intrude on my relationship with Chiara; it was something of mine. Now I can't do that anymore, everything I do has to be put in unity. So, if you wouldn't mind, I could read you this letter that I wrote to Chiara just yesterday.[35]

Chiara Luce realized full well that giving means detaching oneself, losing, being deprived, dispossessing oneself, taking the risk of not having something you might need. Taking that risk with trust, in faith, she discovered great freedom.

In the New Testament, Jesus not only gives freedom to prisoners, but also liberates from every slavery, the slavery of evil and sickness, the pain of oppression, the paralysis caused by guilt.* Indeed, he is shown as the one who gave

---

* See Lk 4:18; Mt 8:16; Mt12:10; Jn 8:11.

himself, placing himself in human hands*. He willingly took on what alienates us, evil and death, to liberate us from them and give us a new heart capable of loving. This is the gift of the new creation that Jesus presents to the world.

The fact that in himself God is "gift" also shines throughout the gospel. Jesus is the "gift of the Father" who has loved us so much that he gave his only Son (Jn 3:16). He welcomes us, his disciples, as a gift, as when he turns to the Father referring to us as "those whom you gave me."† He is "gift" for the Father whose will he wishes to carry out. Everything between him and the Father is reciprocal gift, communion: *"All that is mine is yours, and what is yours is mine"* (Jn 17:10). Even the Spirit is the immeasurable gift that the Father makes to the Son (Jn 3:34). In the good news of Jesus a deeply embedded law is in force, the law of "giving."

Chiara Luce reached an understanding of this profound law, the central core of the gospel. So as to live in the image and likeness of God, she wanted to be gift. The gospel became her point of reference; through giving, she could walk along a stupendous path of life. *"Give and it will be given to you"* (Lk 6:38). This

---

* See 1 Tim 2:6; Ti 2:14.

† See Jn 10:29; 17:6; 18:9.

path is strewn with reciprocal gifts between God and humankind because God never tires of being a gift for those who give and trust in him: *"But to all who received him... he gave power to become children of God"* (Jn 1:12). If we live in his image, he will say to us: "All *that is mine is yours"* (Jn 17:10). He will never fail to manifest his gifts in a thousand ways, and it will be a "hundredfold."*

Chiara Luce was only fourteen years old when she decided for God!

Maker of heaven and earth

At the school of Chiara Lubich, Chiara Badano had learned that everything in creation is reciprocal gift, because all of creation bears the mark of the Trinity.

> The person next to me was created as a gift for me and I was created as a gift for the person next to me. On earth all stands in a relationship of love with all: each thing with each thing. We have to be Love, however, to discover the golden thread among all things that exist.[36]

Each act of "giving" places us into the mystery of the creation of heaven and earth; it unites us to the Creator, the source of our

---

* See Mk 10:30; Lk 8:8

being. Each "gift" is there to perfect and complete creation; it makes us co-creators not only of our own individual stories but also of the story of humankind. It places us into the life of the one God in three Persons who love one another and give all. Giving helps us to enter into the mystery of God's love, who wants us to be creators with him.

Day Seven

A Path of Freedom

In these last few months I have had to work very hard not to use bad language, and the TV often tempts me as well, with films that aren't clean. Every time, I ask special help from Jesus to make it. Unity with the Gen has helped me in the most difficult moments, thinking that they are also going against the current.[37]

*L*iberated in Christ, how can we actually live freedom as Paul invites us (Gal 5:1)? Today's reflection at the school of Chiara Luce will help us to build our freedom by following a sure and speedy path.

For Chiara Luce "cuts" and "pinpricks" were not just words. To maintain the freedom of loving and giving, you cannot simply dispense with the battle against your ego.

She means what she says, because for her whole life she had to struggle through many small battles. She recounts (May 1984, age twelve) an episode when her classmates heard that she attended the Focolare and was a Gen. They began to make fun of her, calling her "the little nun." So she felt rejected, at that age something particularly painful.

> [When] they called me "nun" recently, I didn't know how to react, but in the Mariapolis I found the answer: Him! [Jesus forsaken] The experience of another Gen 3 matched mine exactly. I was happy, I had found the secret.

> [When my classmates] isolated me, I was a bit sad, but I embraced J.F. (= Jesus forsaken) with joy. The next day was our field trip and all my classmates had decided which friend they were going to sit next to on the bus. I was left without anyone—again J.F.! But then on that very morning one of my classmates asked me if I wanted to sit with her because her friend was with another girl, and there it was— the hundredfold![38]

When her mother asked her if she disliked being called "little nun" she answered "no."

> If that's how they see me, it's fine.[39]

Then and there she made the decision:

> ...to love those who are annoying to me.[40]

When she found it difficult to love one of her middle school teachers, she tried twice as hard to smile at him.

> With as much love as possible, I tried to love him, and Jesus saw this sacrifice of mine and immediately rewarded me because, now, whenever I'm distracted and don't say hello to him, he says hello to me, and this gives me the strength to continue loving him all the way to the end and to keep growing.[41]

Strengthened by her faith in God's love, she felt sure that God would respond somehow to her efforts in being faithful to his truth. The good morning greeting from that teacher is what she calls the "hundredfold," and it encouraged her to maintain the approach she had chosen.

During Chiara's freshman year in high school, a teacher remarked to her mother that, in her opinion, her daughter would one day be a lawyer or a judge. Maria Teresa did not understand what the teacher meant, so she asked her daughter, who replied:

> That teacher doesn't believe in God and tries in every way to put the Pope

in a bad light. For example, he criti-
cizes him because he travels too much.
And so I stood up and told him: "I
don't agree with everything you just
said," and I added, "The only reason
the Pope travels is to evangelize the
world."[42]

Adolescence opened a new world, a fasci-
nating world. It was a "crisis" in the root meaning of the word, that is, an important moment
to make a decision, to state a clear judgment
regarding the truth, and to strive to conform
to it through concrete action. Hypocrisy consists in pronouncing such a judgment and then
not following it—, you are lying to yourself
because you are not on the side of the truth..
Adolescence offered Chiara Luce an opportunity to enter into true freedom because she
placed herself in the truth.

She knew where the truth lay, and she knew
that following Jesus and the guidelines of the
Church would require some struggle. Thus her
initial decision, already a radical one, became
even stronger; she committed herself to go all
the way to the end with the "holy journey." In
the spiritual life you cannot settle back and
enjoy the gratification of having reached yesterday's goals. We should never stop pressing
onward until we have made Jesus our own, just

as we have been made his own.* Paul says: *"…
forgetting what lies behind and straining forward to
what lies ahead"* (Phil 3:13). Chiara Luce made
the decision to advance along the path of truth
and freedom. How could she do it in a world
filled with snares, in which it is so easy to just
follow the crowd? Freedom is a gift, yet we find
it difficult to accept, making compromises or
preferring the status quo rather than trying to
free ourselves from what oppresses us.

Chiara Luce could mature and blossom in
freedom above all because of her relationship
with Jesus, her companion on her life adven-
ture.

> Every time, I ask a special grace from
> Jesus.

She shows admirable courage in admitting
the truth, in this case her own inner weakness,
not looking outside of herself for excuses or
extenuating circumstances. She possessed the
clarity to acknowledge her weaknesses openly
and with humility, not only her inner flaws,
but also her behavior toward others, toward
those who sought to help her. This is vitally
important for growth in the spiritual life.

As a child she was truthful.

> You must always believe me, I don't
> tell lies.[43]

---

* See Phil 3:12.

She loved the truth, preferring it to her wounded self-image and pride. Her aunt recounts how one morning when Chiara's parents were away, she slept in. She refused to get up and the aunt threatened to tell her mother. But Chiara replied,

> You don't need to; I'll tell her before you do.[44]

She had the same openness with her Gen 3 assistant.

The feeling that she was linked with others sustained her. She knew she didn't have to struggle alone. Other girls her age were doing the same. The effort asked of her, therefore, also became an act of love, a gift. By struggling against herself she helped others to do the same, a gift that they reciprocated.

She received strength from the strength of the others, and from their sharing. By listening to the experiences of others, she learned how to "go against the current"; she grew. Going against the current can also be an act of love, a gift of oneself.

Day Eight

It's Jesus Forsaken

Two days after Confirmation, I got scarlet fever and had to stay in bed. I missed a whole month of school. This was a hard blow for me, but right away I said to myself: "This is Jesus forsaken for me and I have to love Him as much as possible." And so I began doing lots of acts of love for my parents and, when I was able to get out of bed, for my grandmother who lives upstairs. ...this experience made me redis-cover Jesus forsaken. When I went back to school, I was happy to be able to love Him in my classmates, and I could feel that He was helping me.[45]

*I*n November 1984, she wrote this in a let-ter to a Gen 3 assistant from Genoa. She gives the slight illness and its consequences a name that seems out of proportion to the event: "Jesus forsaken."

Yet here we get to the heart of Chiara Luce's spiritual life, the central theme of these fifteen days of prayer, a theme that this meditation cannot begin to exhaust. We enter into her soul, where God dwells and where she consummated an extraordinary love for Jesus that drew her into the life of God.

Since her first contact with the Focolare, Chiara Luce had encountered this crucified Jesus who cries out his suffering to the Father, asking why he had been forsaken. When Jesus cries, *"My God, my God, why have you forsaken me?"* (Mk 15:34; Mt 27:46), he reveals that he has loved us to the point of giving up his life— not only his physical life, but also what lay in the deepest recesses of his soul and was even more precious: his relationship with the Father.

Feeling separation from the Father was a far more severe laceration, since he had said: *"The Father and I are one"* (Jn 10:30). His suffering was inexpressible, infinite as God, because it is his relationship with the Father that makes him the Son; it is the relationship that confers on him his very identity, his very being. That infinite suffering reveals God's immense love, the love of the Father, Son and Holy Spirit. The Father *"did not spare his own Son"* (Rom 8:32);

he loved the world so much *"that he gave his only Son"* (Jn 3:16). Trinitarian love is revealed on the cross, because Jesus gives us everything, even his intimate life with the Father. The greatest suffering of the Son who obeys the Father is the greatest revelation of their love.

Even when she was very young, Chiara Luce understood this and it fascinated her. There is no age limit for understanding love; children probably understand these things better than adults. In one letter to Chiara Lubich, dated June 1983, Chiara Luce speaks of a rediscovery.

> I re-discovered Jesus forsaken in a special way.

Then she proposes to

> ...see Jesus forsaken as [her] Spouse and to welcome him with joy and especially with as much love as possible.[46]

In response to hearing Jesus' cry, she takes the position of a bride who wants to share her Spouse's fate. She grasped that in his abandonment, Jesus had taken on all our sufferings, whether physical or moral: separations, betrayal, even our sins. Therefore, if he reached out to us in everything that hurts us, it is right and just that we should also meet up with him in each of our sufferings.

In the same letter from 1983 she adds,

> I experienced Him in every neighbor
> that passed by me.

Chiara Lubich writes, *"Every soul is Jesus who cries out in that most painful cry,"*[47] and Chiara Badano found Jesus forsaken in every neighbor, in everything in that neighbor which could annoy her, upset her, even repulse her.

Until November 1984, when the passage at the beginning of this section was written, she found many occasions to recognize him and love him in small sufferings and in the efforts to love those who passed her way. This letter reveals how she had matured; each word is valuable in helping us enter into the dynamism of love for Jesus forsaken, and showing us how to live it ourselves.

Strikingly, she writes *"right away." "I right away said…"* Scarlet fever, a month of school lost: this blow disrupted her plans, her daily life, all that she considered essential. But by this point in her life she had trained herself to see Jesus in all such circumstances, Jesus who in his forsakenness had taken upon himself all of our sufferings:

> This is Jesus forsaken for me and I
> should love him as much as I can.

"For me." What most people would consider an unforeseen suffering she, instead, found a visit from Jesus. She understands how to change a negative sign into a positive. She gladly welcomes Jesus' visit and wants to love him.

We have already seen how Chiara Luce recognized "Jesus forsaken" in the mocking laughter of her classmates. When she felt marginalized she would only say, *"It's him."*

Thus the meaning of personal pain can change; it can become God's nearness. This does not mean loving pain, but loving the One who has taken it on himself. It requires that we not try to escape from suffering—which would be our natural instinct—but to stand firm and look into the face of the One who embraced it fully, and in our turn embrace him as a spouse.

"I should love him as much as possible." This is precisely the logic of Pascal, who in his famous *Pensées* writes: *"Jesus will be in agony until the end of the world, we must not sleep during that time."* In all the sufferings of the world Jesus raises his cry of forsakenness; we should not leave him alone, but take up the suffering and share it with him, or better, strive to offer him relief by being happy to be with him.

"And so I began doing lots of acts of love for my parents and, when I was able to get out of bed, for my grandmother who lives upstairs." When he pays us

a "visit" we feel specially chosen by the King, able to love. We share the sufferings of Jesus and he shares with us his Spirit of Love. Our hearts widen and we become creative in making the people around us feel love.

"This experience made me rediscover Jesus forsaken." The more Chiara Luce loved, the more she knew the One she loved, and the more he revealed himself to her; her coming to know him was a source of light, gladness and joy. *"When I went back to school, I was happy to be able to love Him in my classmates,"* she says. Love between Jesus and us becomes reciprocal, an unfailing fountain, like the water that Jesus asks for, and wants to give to the Samaritan woman.

On this eighth day of prayer let us recall the first days of these meditations, when Chiara Luce invited us to open wide our hearts and ears to the cry of Jesus within us and in all of humankind. Jesus' cry resounds throughout the ages, announcing God's betrothal to humanity in Jesus Christ. Out of love he took on all our suffering by experiencing within himself separation from the very source of his being.

Day Nine

My Life Has Been Transformed

These past few days have been a bit difficult for me, because following the move to Savona several problems have arisen such as the school and feeling homesick for Sassello, that I love so much. I realized it was a countenance of Jesus forsaken. It was hard for me to say yes to Him, but I tried, giving my mother a hand with the final arrangements, studying my lessons because it was the will of God, renewing my commitment each morning to the "holy journey." My life was transformed, and then the news that there were Gen 3 meetings seemed to me a special help from Jesus for me to remain "up" all the time.[48]

*W*elcoming Jesus in suffering, the suffering that touches me right now, today, here and now, the suffering of the world: this is what Chiara Luce offers as a truth within the reach of every person, a new way of looking at the world. Chiara Luce persevered in discovering this truth, in going deeper into her choice, because life in union with Jesus forsaken is always new. His many countenances are always new, at times shocking and contradictory. But when we can recognize him, we go from discovery to discovery, from understanding to understanding.

A letter to Chiara Lubich from November 1983 is connected to the letter cited above:

> The most important thing for me during this convention has been the rediscovery of Jesus forsaken. Before, I lived it in a rather superficial way and accepted him in expectation of the joy there would come. In this convention I realized that I was doing it all wrong. I shouldn't have exploited him, but loved him and that's all. I discovered that Jesus forsaken is the key to unity with God and I want to choose him as my first spouse and prepare myself for the moment when he comes. To prefer him![49]

"In expectation of the joy." Chiara Luce understands the lurking danger of looking for the

joy that flows from love for Jesus forsaken, rather than uniting with him in suffering and with him, drinking the chalice to the dregs. Embracing Jesus forsaken is a source of happiness when that embrace is sincere. In your love for Jesus crucified you cannot cheat. You need to look him in the face, not turning away from his suffering: *"They will look on the one whom they have pierced"* (Jn 19:37).

True love is a burning desire to be consumed in one with the beloved. It involves a basic choice–choosing a spouse. Jesus forsaken has already espoused humanity in all of its suffering and pain, including sin.[*] Since he never chose among the vast variety of sufferings, neither should his spouse; we should share everything with him, prepare for his arrival, prefer him.

"Prefer him." Following Chiara Lubich, Chiara Badano uses this phrase. Let me repeat: it is not a matter of loving the suffering, and even less of preferring it, but of preferring Jesus who in his forsakenness has clothed himself with that suffering. Putting up with him reluctantly or giving him a cold welcome would not be love.

This radical choice is then demonstrated by remaining faithful to it in daily life, in small

---

[*] See 2 Cor 5:21.

and big things, as the opening quote states. That passage is from a letter to her Gen 3 assistant written in 1985. Chiara Luce doesn't manage or rather, is no longer able to say her yes *immediately*, but her yes is translated into deeds, into a willed effort to overcome suffering, to forget herself in order to love.

> It was hard for me to say yes to Him, but I tried, giving my mother a hand... studying my lessons because it was the will of God, renewing my commitment each morning to the "holy journey." [50]

In another letter to a Gen 3 friend, written on July 14, 1986, she does not try to hide the effort it took, during the setbacks of life, to unite herself to Jesus on the cross:

> As you know I failed the year in school and that was a huge suffering for me. I didn't manage to give this suffering immediately to Jesus. It took me a long time to recover a little and still today, at times, when I think of it, I feel like crying. It's Jesus forsaken! [51]

As a child, in the excitement of being able to love Jesus, she made a sincere, generous choice, a choice made in love. When she realized that great effort would be required in everyday life to remain faithful to that choice, she again said yes, with her whole will. She based her entire life on this cornerstone.

But God is faithful, so faithful that he intro-duced her into a new dimension:

My life was transformed.

It was transformed because God gave her a deeper knowledge of his love, made her taste the sweetness and tenderness of union with him: *"I discovered that Jesus forsaken is the key to unity with God."* Unity with God and knowl-edge of God go hand in hand: *"They shall all know me, from the least of them to the greatest;"** *"And they shall all be taught by God"* (Jn 6:25).

From this mutual faithfulness—between God and Chiara Luce—a deeper love poured out of her heart for the people around her. Love for Jesus forsaken on the cross pushes us out toward our brothers and sisters, to understand them, to take on their sufferings. The fact is— we must never lose sight of this– that for Chiara Luce loving means loving the neighbor whom we see, whomever that may be, loving them in God and for God whom we cannot see.

In the Incarnation, the Word became one of us so as to make us children of God. In the same way, love for Jesus on the cross leads us to reproduce his style of loving, that is, to "descend" to where our brother or sister is in order to "rise again" with them and introduce

---

* See Heb 8:11.

them with us into the life of God. "Making yourself one," becoming the other, could seem like abasement, an impoverishment, but in reality it is an increase of love, an enrichment. Chiara Luce had learned Jesus forsaken's art of loving; she allowed herself to be "infected" with his style of love.

Emptied of his divinity, he taught her to silence thoughts and attachments, even to set aside inspirations in order to make herself one with her neighbors, which meant serving them and loving them. This type of love is a sharing in the very life of God who is Love, and it builds up the community of believers, the Church.

Whenever we recognize the concrete presence of Jesus on the cross hidden behind any personal suffering or behind the sufferings of the world, and whenever in our own small way we strive to alleviate that suffering, everything acquires meaning. Our vision of reality becomes positive and prophetic.

Day Ten

Beyond the Wound

I'm delighted that you went to the Gen convention and, as you say, since the meeting caused you a bit of hardship, precisely for this reason it was truly beautiful.

Overcoming suffering makes us free.

Reading your letter brought to my mind many memories of my first Gen conventions; I particularly remember one near Rome, when I was nine years old [1981]. It was very deep and decisive, but also with some moments of Jesus forsaken to offer to our Spouse! Chiara [Lubich] tells us that each time a suffering presents itself we should go "beyond the wound." This was our proposal, wasn't it? It's really our way.[52]

L ife is transformed through love for Jesus in his forsakenness on the cross; our vision of the world changes, as if by a divine alchemy. For, as Chiara Lubich says, "...the cross bears a God...[and so], your redemption was full and overflowing."[53]

Having learned to say yes even when she didn't feel like it, Chiara Badano knew how to face the great trial of her illness. In an ongoing and heroic manner, she would repeat her yes to the One she considered her Spouse.

It was March, 1989. Maria Teresa tells of Chiara Luce's return from the hospital when her daughter, having undergone chemotherapy for the first time, learned the seriousness of her illness.

> The pain was written on her face. She threw herself on the bed...and closed her eyes. I didn't know how I should act. I asked her: "Do you want to talk about it? Aren't you going to tell me anything?" She answered: *"No, not now."* She remained lying on the bed for twenty-five minutes, and then she called me. She had her usual radiant smile. She told me: *"Now you can talk."* A month later Chiara confessed to me that those had been the hardest, most dramatic moments in her life; that during those few minutes she had been able to say her yes to Jesus,

who was asking her for something big,
something more.

Then came the moment—she told
me—when she "had to identify herself
with Jesus forsaken, just as she had
learned from Chiara Lubich."[54]

Identify with Jesus forsaken: this is what
Chiara Luce did during those dramatic twenty-
five minutes. From then on, she would gather
the sweet fruits of union with God, as she had
never experienced before:

Now I live in a very intense relationship with Jesus, one that you could
never even imagine.[55]

Her love for each person grew deeper and
more delicate. Everyone she met or who came
to visit her was struck by the light that radiated
from her face, to the point that some people
thought that she was the one living the real life,
and everybody else, the ones who were in good
health, were living in darkness.

When she was writing the letter cited at the
beginning of this chapter to her fellow Gen
2, Daniela Cerati, she had already become a
true master in the art of living with Jesus forsaken and loving him. She could look back
on her experience and draw the correct con-
clusions: *"It's really our way,"* it's the path that
characterizes us. Then she writes this mag-

nificent sentence: *"Overcoming suffering makes us FREE." Nailed* to her bed, almost totally dependent on others, Chiara Luce experiences great freedom.

Jesus forsaken is the way that leads us to God and allows us, with our brothers and sisters, to build up the body of Christ—if we know how to go "beyond the wound." This expression of Chiara Lubich's means having a love for Jesus forsaken that is so strong and true that the Risen Lord shines out in us.

"Jesus forsaken," writes Chiara Lubich, *"embraced, locked to one's self, wanted as our only all, he consumed in one with us, we consumed in one with him, made suffering with him Suffering: here lies everything. Here is how we become (by participation) God, Love."*[56] Loving Jesus forsaken with this measure of love makes us share in the greatest mutation in human history, the resurrection of Jesus. Chiara Luce desired this Jesus as her everything in life:

> I notice that God asks something more of me, something greater. Perhaps I'll be on this bed for years…I don't know. I'm only interested in God's will, to do that well, in the present moment: to stay in the game, in God's game, to play along with God.

No longer does she say "Your will be done," but instead she wants with all her heart what her Spouse wants.

> Yes, I too repeat with you: "If you want it, Jesus, I want it too." There's still something else I wanted to tell you: here, everyone is asking for a miracle (and you know how much I want it!). But I can't ask for it. I think this difficulty I'm having in asking him for it is because I don't think it enters into His Will. Could that be it? What do you think?[58]

Chiara Luce had two attitudes toward suffering which on a rational level would seem impossible to reconcile, but in the regime of love are actually one. She wanted to unite herself to Jesus in his suffering, she wanted to be with him in what hurts him, she wanted this with the all the strength of her will. But at the same time and with the same force of will, she knows and believes she will meet the Risen Jesus who has already transformed this evil that touches her and those around her, mended this tear and restored peace.

She believed that the Risen Lord is already within the Forsaken Lord, in embryonic form. It was enough to live in him, choosing him as her one desire in life, gathering the fruits of his death and resurrection, and giving him the joy of seeing that his suffering was not in vain. By maintaining these two opposites that actually are one we are able to be "beyond the wound," to live with him his death and resurrection—or better, his resurrection within his death.

Nevertheless, this love is never achieved once and for all; it must be reconstructed continually, because the countenances of Jesus forsaken are many. Chiara Luce never rested on what she lived yesterday, but each day began again to go beyond the wound in an active interplay of death and resurrection. In each present moment, love allowed her to catch a glimpse of the next step. And this love made her encounter the Risen Lord. The face of Jesus forsaken is certainly that of suffering, but Jesus forsaken is God.

At the end of her life she could say,

> I no longer ask Jesus to come and take me, because it might seem that I don't want to suffer. Instead, I still want to offer this suffering to Jesus and to bear his cross with him.[59]

Her words express the breadth and truth of that article of the Creed: *"I believe in Jesus Christ…who suffered under Pontius Pilate, was crucified, died and was buried: descended into hell; on the third day he rose again."*

Chiara Luce had centered her life on the core of the Christian faith, because the object of Christian "belief" is always the resurrection, the power of God transforming death into life.

Day Eleven

Chiara Luce's Faith

After meeting Chiara Luce it was normal to ask yourself deep questions and examine how you are living your faith. This is what happened to me, but I know for a fact that I was not the only one who had to compare the way they lived with the life she transmitted.[60]

If young people had even just a speck of your faith, the Church would be saved.[61]

"Our roles are reversed. Now you are a mother for me." I was referring to her example, and in particular to the witness to the faith she was giving to me.[62]

After having verified that her daughter had indeed died...Maria Teresa began to recite the Creed, and all of us joined in with her.[63]

*W*ith her way of being, her way of living and dying, Chiara Luce was a special witness to the faith—as everyone who knew her said. The declarations cited in the quotes above are quite convincing. Under the aspect of the faith, Chiara Badano is perfectly in tune with the New Testament, where faith is so central that it is mentioned more often than love. Weren't Jesus' disciples referred to as "believers"?

Let us consider a few examples of belief in the writings of St. Paul and St. John.

St. Paul tells us that "through faith" we were saved, have life, are justified,* become heirs of God (Rm 4:20), children of God (Gal 3:26). But what is the meaning of the words, "through faith"?

To put it very simply, for Paul, the object of faith is always the resurrection of Jesus and consists in holding to the truth of his death for our sins and his resurrection for our justification (Rm 5:25). But it is not enough to hold these things to be true. We need to appropriate this reality for ourselves by accepting the means through which the justification-filiation was given to us: Christ's ignominious death on the cross. There he assumed completely

---

* See Rm 3:22, 28, 30.

our condition as human beings, to the point of being "clothed" in our separation from God.

It is necessary to enter freely into the scandal of his humiliation where, paradoxically, all his power is disclosed, into his apparent foolishness that is wiser than human beings.[*] It would be counter intuitive to enter into the truth of Jesus' death and resurrection—which transformed the world and human history— and not live in communion with his death in the small sufferings of daily life so as to be raised with him.

Sharing in Jesus' Passover means giving to God the joy of seeing that his gifts are not being wasted but are allowed to come to fruition. Since God has reconciled us to himself in Christ, then let us reconcile with God, as Paul begs us to do.[†] This is precisely what happens to us in baptism, which is the outward sign of this new life that has been given to us (Rm 6:4-5).

Seen from the Pauline perspective, the life and death of Chiara Luce are filled with teaching. By recognizing and embracing Jesus in his forsakenness, she confessed her faith in the Risen Lord and lived already risen with Christ (Eph 2:6); she participated in the pow-

---

* See 1 Cor 1:21-25.
† 2 Cor 5:20; Rm 5:6-11.

erful action of his death and resurrection, experiencing fully the reality of justification and filiation. Through her embrace of the Crucified-Forsaken Lord, "she allowed herself to be reconciled with God" and lived fully the covenant with him in reciprocity.

Chiara Luce did not want anything from his redemption to be wasted; she wanted to assure him that it was not in vain.

> Mamma, it was a terrible night, but I didn't waste a single moment, because I offered everything to Jesus.[64]

In line with this desire to waste nothing of the redemption, while praying with her mother, she made her own the words of Chiara Lubich that have also been put to music: *"Here I am, Jesus, before you again today, all new, just as you want me to be. I will be the answer to your 'Why?' a worthy fruit of your abandonment. Here I am!"*[65]

In John's Gospel, written so that we might believe,[*] the attitude of "belief" marks the boundary between light and darkness. John says that when our faith is authentic we already have eternal life: *"Whoever believes in him may have eternal life."* (Jn 3:15[†]); we are made sons and daughters, *"To all who received him, who believed in his name, he gave power to become*

---

[*] See Jn 20:31.

[†] See also 5:24; 6:47-50.

children of God" (Jn 1:12). In John, "to receive Jesus" is synonymous with believing that he is the Son. Moreover, authentic "belief" makes us sharers in God's glory: *"If you believed, you would see the glory of God"* (Jn 11:40). Authentic faith also secures our happiness (Jn 20:29).

In the Gospel of John, the "hour" is that time when Jesus will *"depart from this world and go to the Father"* (Jn 13:1). It is the hour of the cross when all the signs are changed and reality is transformed, just as the water changed into wine at the wedding feast of Cana was an anticipation of this hour. Jesus even says it: *"Woman, what concern is that to you and to me? My hour has not yet come"* (Jn 2:4). Anyone who gazes with authentic faith and love upon the cross of the one who has loved us is transformed and healed from evil, a healing of which he is the sign—exactly like the serpent that Moses raised up in the desert healed those who had been bitten by a serpent. In John's Gospel, Jesus' cross is the hour of his glorification.

For John, faith is essentially a loving encounter with Christ. "Believing" means encountering Jesus and loving him. *"If you love me, you will keep my commandments"* (Jn 14:15). *"Do you love me?"* (Jn 12:17).

During her stay in the hospital, when the archbishop asked her the reason for her radiant smile, she replied simply:

I try to love Jesus.[66]

This fits in with Johannine faith. Chiara Luce strove to believe in his love and to remain in him, her eyes fixed on him, sharing in his suffering. This demonstrates how mortal illness can be transformed into a sign of life and resurrection. Chiara Luce was an authentic witness of Jesus' words: *"Those who believe in me, even though they die will live"* (Jn 11:25).

How simple and stupendous was Chiara Luce's faith! With St. John we can sum it up with a single statement: Chiara Luce had a burning love for Jesus; she had followed him along his path of return to the Father. With St. Paul we can say that although close to death, she rose with Christ *"through faith in the power of God, who raised him from the dead"* (Col 2:12). She is an authentic witness to the truth of the Word of the living God.

This is the faith that Jesus asks of us, the faith that the first Christians teach us and that the New Testament testifies to, a faith that moves mountains and makes us throw ourselves into the life of God.

Day Twelve

Wisdom and Light

*H*er last stay in the hospital coincided with a convention for Gen 2 leaders in Castel Gandolfo, Italy.

One morning I was feeling particularly sick. I knew that on that same day, Silvana* and the Gen were going to pray a consenserint† for me. I wanted to unite myself with them, too, and so my mother and I joined them in their prayer. Since this is the

_____

* Silvana Veronesi, one of Chiara Lubich's early companions, was in charge of the Gen girls at that time.

† The *consenserint* is a form of prayer commonly used in the Movement, based on Matthew 18:19: "If two of you agree on earth about anything you ask, it will be done for you by my Father in heaven." *"Consenserint"* (from Latin words meaning "to consent" or "agree") suggests a "we" praying in unity.

year of the Holy Spirit, besides asking to be cured I also asked the Eternal Father to illuminate the facilitators of the meeting, and I asked for wisdom and light for all the Gen.

It was really a moment of God. Physically, I was suffering a lot, but my soul was singing. We continued praying for quite a while, so that this moment would not pass.[67]

Chiara Luce Badano's spiritual life had been following a linear path, but in the illness that led to her death it took a qualitative leap into a new dimension. The transformation brought about in her, which resembled at times a transfiguration, was the working of the Holy Spirit who burst forth from Christ on the cross, the Spirit that Jesus commended to the Father (*"Father, into your hands I commend my spirit"* Lk 23:46), the same Spirit given in all its fullness to anyone who unites himself or herself to the sufferings of Jesus. Through her yes, she entered into a new dimension, the dimension of Pentecost.

The Holy Spirit burst forth in her the God who does nothing else but unite and love, and is the link of love between the Father and the Son. He had taken possession of her soul so fully that it seemed Chiara Luce was no longer alone in living and dying; animated by the

Spirit, she did nothing else but create bonds with people, kindling and strengthening relationships. At this point she did nothing else but love, inspiring a return of love, an atmosphere of love. It was no longer "I" living in her, but rather "we."

In this context, let us re-read the December 20, 1989, letter to Chiara Lubich that was cited in the introduction. She calls Chiara Lubich "Mamma," giving further evidence of the deepening bond between them. Chiara Luce and her mother unite themselves to the spirit of the convention in Rome. Chiara Luce, Maria Teresa, the Gen—all together pronounce a prayer in unity, uttered by "we," a community.

Love personified had made a triumphal entry into her soul, bringing to her gifts of understanding, peace and joy. Her suffering was immersed in Love. Because she knew the sweetness and tenderness of the Consoler Spirit, she could truthfully write:

> Physically, I was suffering a lot, but my soul was singing.

> The Spirit brought into the clay vessel of her wounded, weakened, and decaying body the gift of love: "Now, nothing healthy is left in me, but I still have my heart and with that I can still love"[68]

During that year, members of the Focolare had been studying and meditating upon the theme of the Holy Spirit. Chiara Luce had experienced the Spirit coming into her soul, something she continued to long for. She preferred above all else the prayer: *"Come, Holy Spirit, come! And from your celestial home, shed a ray of light divine!"* One day, after a priest had brought Holy Communion to her and was already on his way out the door, she called him back to say "the prayer" to the Holy Spirit* with her.[69]

Each word of that prayer was like a balm for both soul and body and gave her the strength to carry on loving until the end: "Come, Father of the poor! Come source of all our store...shine within these hearts of yours."

The Spirit of wisdom helped her to perceive the meaning of her life. She tasted the sweetness of wisdom when, realizing the seriousness of her illness and saying yes, she was able to see beyond. As did the man born blind, all of us have to regain our sight, and Chiara Luce, with her yes, opened her eyes. What did she see? As her mother testifies, she understood God's plan for her life:

---

* See the words of the prayer: Come Holy Spirit on page 127.

I felt Chiara was interpreting and understanding the suffering that God called her to, as a fruit of a lengthy preparation. She even said that, without her realizing it, Jesus had prepared her in the preceding years to endure this great suffering.[70]

By then, she was also able to recognize the shadows that obscure wisdom's light:

Oh, how I would have loved to stop that train that was taking me further and further away! But I still didn't understand. I was still too absorbed by insignificant, futile and passing things. Another world was waiting for me, and all I had to do was abandon myself to it. But now I feel enveloped in a splendid plan which is being revealed to me, little by little.[71]

The same light that revealed a splendid plan made her see her illness as a gift from God;[72] it made her realize that it arrived at the right moment. She said to her mother:

The illness arrived at the right moment, otherwise perhaps I would have been lost.[73]

Didn't Jesus himself consider his suffering and death to be necessary?*

---

* See Lk 24:26.

That is why, for anyone who has taken up the holy journey with her, she could think of nothing better to ask for than "wisdom and light." And how she wished that this Spirit would be poured out over everyone!

Before a large youth event organized by the Gen on March 26, 1990, she wrote to them:

> I offer you my nothingness so that the Holy Spirit might bestow on all the young people His gifts of love, light and peace, so that they may all understand what a free and immense gift life is, and how very important it is to live each moment of it in the fullness of God.[74]

"Give us your seven holy gifts." The spirit of fortitude that she called upon assisted her in every moment. The spirit of piety helped her to love Jesus and to offer him her life in preparation for her marriage to him. The spirit of intellect made her recognize the visits of her Spouse:

> I feel so small and the road ahead so hard, I often feel overwhelmed by pain. But it's my Spouse who comes to visit me, isn't it?[75]

I believe in the Holy Spirit

The Spirit of love of the Father and of the Son is the *"most blessed light divine"* that fills the heart of his faithful. Chiara Badano was filled with the light of the Holy Spirit; even the name given to her by Chiara Lubich means "light" (Luce). Nothing could have been more appropriate.

United to Jesus, the light of the world,[*] she projected and radiated a beam of light that, according to her own bishop's testimony, leaves one *"blinded by her clear, pure spirit."*[76] Could a better vocation exist than being called to be a *"source of light in the world"*?[†]

---

[*] See Jn 9:5.
[†] See Phil 2:15.

Day Thirteen

A People on a Journey

Mamma, I'm ashamed to write this note to you and don't think that, even though I had the courage to act as I did, I don't regret it. I do regret it—a lot! (I almost can't sleep)!

I can't find the courage to ask for your forgiveness for the umpteenth time. Mamma, I promise, (and I don't know if I'll be able to do it, so I ask you to help me and call me every time you see me going to my room. I'll try not to grumble!) I promise to clear the table like I did in Varazze. I don't want to make you suffer like that anymore. I'm lazy, I know! But I'll try not to be. Punish me tomorrow—it's only right, I truly deserve it.[77]

*T*his note may have been written in autumn 1988, after Chiara Luce had been stricken with the illness, and she had refused to help her mother clean up the kitchen after lunch and closed herself in her room because she was so tired. In any case, this note is a masterpiece of sensitivity and delicate love.

Chiara succeeds in putting herself in her mother's place, so much so that she even dictates what her mother's actions should be: *"Help me, call me, and punish me."* She forgets herself completely; she loves—period. Chiara Luce could grow and unite herself to Jesus because she loved, and by loving she developed the virtues. She took on the suffering she may have provoked in others as well as the suffering they may have caused her. In doing so, she transformed her own errors and those of others into love, just like Jesus who took our sins upon himself and transformed them into love toward the Father.

While bedridden she asked forgiveness for the smallest things.[78] She asked forgiveness from her mother and her aunt *"for having lacked in charity."*[79] When a doctor who examined her in her last hours said something that hurt her, she forgave him. She not only forgave him, but wanted to give him one of her books.[80] Whenever she heard someone being criticized, she never judged but only said: *"God will judge."*[81]

One day her mother asked: *"Are you suffering a lot?"* She smiled and answered,

> Jesus is using bleach to remove all my stains. The bleach burns, but it removes all the black spots. Then when I go to heaven, I'll be as white as snow.[82]

Her words show that she knows God is acting in her. Through her sufferings, whether due to her physical pain, her sense of being very small, or her difficulty in abiding in love, she recognizes God accomplishing his plan of love. What's expected of her, her only task, is to love and let God do his work, with unconditional trust and total abandonment.

We have highlighted her abandonment to God's action, both in moments of strength as well as in weakness, and her constantly beginning again to love, in order to introduce what the church was for her. In fact, the church in which Chiara Luce moved toward the encounter with the Spouse—the domestic church, the local church and the ecclesial movement to which she belonged—was a people on a journey toward unity and holiness.

This church, always in need of purification, grows and is strengthened through reciprocal communion, where each member places himself or herself in an attitude of listening to the others. For example, Chiara Luce longed that those who had gone to heaven ahead of her could teach her how to die. Alberto and Carlo, two boys from near Genoa who also were Focolare members, shared a deep bond with each other. They had both died at the age of twenty.

On August 18, 1980, Alberto died in a mountain-climbing accident. The very next day Carlo Grisolia, whom Chiara Lubich called "Vir" (man of strength), was hospitalized with a fast-growing tumor that led to his death in a little over a month. The cause for their beatification and canonization was opened in 2008. The unprecedented step was taken of treating their process as a single cause—two friends who belonged to the same group of young people from the Focolare and who shared a single desire to live with Jesus in their midst.[*]

Chiara Luce fervently desired to hear directly from Carlo's own mother how he had lived the illness that took his life. So Carlo's mother told her about those forty days of her son's illness, how he offered his sufferings for the church, often repeating the words of Chiara Lubich: *"I have only one Spouse on earth."*[83] His motto became *"I live to meet Jesus,"* another

---

[*] See Mt 18:20.

phrase he learned from Chiara Lubich. As the end drew closer, Carlo's desire to unite himself to Jesus grew more and more: *"It's wonderful to go and meet Jesus,"* he said. *"I want to belong totally to God!"*

Carlo (Vir's) death fascinated Chiara Badano. On July 19, 1990, she wrote to Chiara Lubich:

> This evening my heart is full of joy. Do you know why? Vir's mom came to see me. It was a very strong moment of Jesus in our midst…. Oh, Mamma, will I also manage to be faithful to J. F. [Jesus Forsaken] and live for that encounter with him as Vir did?[84]

Chiara Luce's death, which could be described as a death of love and in love, was the fruit of an entire community:

> I feel very strongly your unity, your sacrifices and your prayers that allow me to plunge into the Holy Journey, renewing my yes moment by moment.[85]

When thanked for her offering, she responded:

> I don't really do anything at all! On the contrary, it's all of you who are a help for me.[86]

She wrote to a *focolarino**

> Your consecration, which is an authentic expression of your love for God, helps me to be faithful to Jesus forsaken.[87]

On May 25, 1990, she wrote to a Gen:

> Thanks again for the prayers and sacrifices. They're *so important!* If I didn't feel this strong unity that binds us together, I'd never be able to carry on.[88]

In her final hours she never stopped giving thanks, something that amazed her father, Ruggero.

> My daughter's behavior seemed impossible to me: with such joy and simplicity she [was able] to greet [her visitors] and thank [them] for their support and for the prayers they were constantly offering for her.[89]

One day at the hospital, Chiara and her parents read and meditated on a message from Chiara Lubich, and then shared with each other what was deep in their soul. Chiara Luce shared how she had offered *"the suffering caused by the pump and the chemotherapy,"* and then

---

* Focolarino: member of the core community of men or women who consecrate their lives to God for the goals of the Focolare Movement.

right afterward she almost exploded with joy because of how happy they were:

> Whenever we have Jesus among us like this, we are the happiest family in the world.[90]

Ruggero commented:

> And that was true, because despite such a tragic situation, I was serene and I remember that Chiara was singing at the top of her voice.[91]

"Chiara wanted to say," Maria Teresa observed, "that our happiness came from the Holy Spirit who was present in our midst because we were loving one another"[92]

Sharing one's own efforts at living the Christian life is a sign of great love and trust, and when you manage to do that, Jesus, his Spirit, and the church are present.

This may have been what Bishop Maritano understood one day as he left Chiara Luce's room. Maria Teresa remembers him commenting, *"We are asking everyone for it, but as for me? I've already seen the miracle."* When asked what he meant, he explained: *"Looking at you three."*[93] He had witnessed the miracle of the living Church, of the Spirit of Jesus working. He had personally experienced "the home and school of communion."[94]

Day Fourteen

Wherever Mutual Love Reigns

We are one body. It's like with me, if it hurts in one place right now, I feel it all over and so I have to act in such a way that I never flee from the grace of Jesus, so that I don't cause harm to all the others. We're linked, we're one.[95]

There is no longer Jew or Greek, there is no longer slave or free, there is no longer male and female; for all of you are one in Christ Jesus.

(Gal 3:28).

"*O*ne in Christ Jesus" means "one person," a single subject. With Chiara

Luce we continue to be plunged into the innermost reality of the church, the Body of Christ.

Paraphrasing the apostle Paul, one could say that among the friends who went to support Chiara there was no longer the one who was sick or the one who was healthy, in the Badano family there was no longer father or mother or daughter, for all were projected into each other and were "one person."

In order to live out this oneness in Christ Jesus, Chiara Luce began to multiply the pacts, those explicit mutual agreements that each person makes to live in Jesus' love in order to help and support one another. Gianfranco Piccardo, who was on his way to Africa, testifies:

> I made a pact with Chiara. I told her I would offer the difficulties I would encounter in Africa for her; and she would offer her sufferings for me. This was a powerful pact that always stayed with me.[96]

To a priest who went to visit her, Chiara Luce declared:

> With God's help I'm ready to give my life for you.[97]

indicating the pact of mutual love, based on the new commandment of Jesus, that we love one another *"as he has loved us."**

This one body into which Chiara Luce has been inserted is nourished with one bread, the Eucharist, Jesus' supreme gift of his body and blood. In a people on the journey to holiness, where each person tries, in his or her own daily life, to share in the passion, death and resurrection of Jesus, to give themselves sincerely to others and to serve them, this sacrament becomes the sign of something that already exists in their lives. Therefore, what the Eucharist expresses can be fully accomplished, that is, to be the sign and means of the union of each individual with the death and resurrection of Christ and of the union among all.

The Eucharist is "thanksgiving," infinite gratitude, and implies that everything is "gift," both Jesus who gives himself in his body and his blood, and our response in love, expressed in our conscious sharing in this gift. There is no doubt that the Eucharist was the peak moment in Chiara Luce's life, what gave meaning to everything. She ardently desired receiving it. *"I'm really happy you came,"* she told a priest who unannounced brought her Holy Communion.

---

* See Jn 13:34; 15:12.

All morning I've been saying: "Come,
Lord Jesus," and you've brought him
to me.[98]

*"I have to act in such a way that I never flee from
the grace of Jesus, so that I don't cause harm to all the
others."* For Chiara Luce, "the grace of Jesus" is
her illness; it is Jesus who in his love wants her
with him on the cross. She wants to accept this
love and follow it with active passivity, in the
footsteps of Mary, who allowed God's work to
be accomplished in her: *"Let it be with me according to your word"* (Lk 1:38).

The Badano family, a small domestic
church, tried to allow God to act, not posing
any resistance to the "grace of Jesus." Maria
Teresa helped her daughter to remain in God,
to do his will; she reminded her of the deci-
sions she had made, in a relationship that was
not only filial and maternal, but also spiritual.
She offered up her daughter and her own inexpressible pain as she watched Chiara Luce die.

Chiara Luce did not want attention; she
put herself last, once saying to her mom:
*"Remember, Mamma, before me there was
Daddy."*[99] Nor was it any different for Ruggero
when, feeling excluded from the relationship
between his wife and his daughter because of
their close spiritual affinity, he found a way of
transforming this suffering into prayer:

The first few times I was hurt: Chiara had asked me to go away and leave them alone. Then I realized it wasn't a matter of a lack of trust in me and, thereafter, in moments such as those I would pray so that the presence of Jesus among them would be even stronger. I prayed that he would go to be with them in my place.[100]

Ruggero lived the emptiness of love into which the Holy Spirit could enter and work, renewing relationships, renewing life.

Each of those around Chiara Luce received and gave, reassured and offered advice. Chiara Luce told a focolarino the night before he took his perpetual vows:

> Don't worry, I'm living all for you. Go ahead, you're ready![101]

When someone asked her what to do with the money she had given to him, she responded:

> Listen to the voice of the Holy Spirit, He'll tell you.[102]

Her mother told her: *"We'll be lost when you're gone. What will I do?"* She answered:

> Follow God, then you will have done everything.[103]

Living for the sanctification of this Body, Chiara Luce had every right to call herself the bride of the One who "loved the church and gave himself up for her" (Eph 5:25). Therefore, she prepared for her death and funeral as for a wedding. Before becoming his personal bride, Chiara went out to meet Christ, the spouse of the church, and she lived fully what it means to be "the church-spouse." The living church that loves and believes, in which Chiara Luce lived in order to meet Jesus, was described by St. Bonaventure as "the mutual love event."[104] It is this love that binds all together, and is, according to the circumstances, giving, or welcoming the gift, serving or gratitude. It is a church that reproduces the image of Mary, the Mother of Jesus, the person who, more than anyone else, collaborates in the redemption, having lived in an exceptional way the mystery of Christ, from the Incarnation to Pentecost.

Even before the passion and death of her Son, Mary lived deeply her own abandonment. The gospel shows Jesus, her own son, rejecting her several times. *"Woman, what do you want from me?"* (Jn 2:4). Indeed, throughout her entire life she, the one *"who believed"* (Lk 1:45), had been trained in faith by her Son. She is the true disciple. At the foot of the cross, the "full of grace" becomes the "full of faith." She believed that in his passion her son fully manifested God's yes to humanity, taking on the sufferings of every human being.

Mary is also the icon of humanity's response, welcoming and uniting itself to the redemption, thus allowing it to come to its greatest fruition. A bond between mother and child was certainly formed between Mary and Chiara Luce, because Chiara Luce, a disciple of Jesus in the faith, also placed herself at the service of the redemption.

Thus, in a community where each member participates in the Paschal mystery, according to whatever God asks of them, the mystery of Mary, the Mother of believers is lived out. In such a community there is a mother's heart for humanity that is forever thirsting for its God and for the Mother of God.[105]

Day Fifteen

Abundant Fruit

I want this relationship of mutual love and unity to begin and grow with others, so that happiness will be multiplied and in this way God will be in our midst.[106]

Be happy because I am.[107]

*C*hiara Luce grew up in a church that has a mission, and she participates fully in the challenges presented to the church by the world. In November 1985, when she was still very young, she wrote to Chiara Lubich, *"I've offered every second of this day for the Synod,"*[108] referring to the synod of bishops convoked on the twentieth anniversary of the Second Vatican Council.

She felt Jesus' fervent desire to bring back together his lost children (Jn 11:5). She knew the path he had followed to bring humankind into unity. She knew that in his abandonment he united himself with every person, and that in him every person could find the model for bringing unity, in some small way, to the world around them so that people could experience what unity is, the source of pure happiness.

United to her "almighty Spouse,"[109] Chiara Luce lived for the unity of all humanity with God and with one another. She had a weakness for those who experienced separation, and tried to reunite them. From the time she was small, she helped to restore peace between her mother and grandmother.[110] Even when her illness was quite advanced, she invited a couple experiencing difficulty in their marriage to watch with her a film version of Richard Bach's *Jonathan Livingston Seagull*, in order to help herself as well as them to fly high, conquering everything with love.[111] In short, she did all that she could, even if it was small, so that the piece of humanity around her would be a people gathered in the unity of the Father, of the Son, and of the Holy Spirit.[112]

She lived and prayed that everyone involved in her life might be true to the way of life that they had chosen. She invited the young people of the Focolare to live in a radical way,[113] and also would have liked to include in that "way" every young person in the whole world.

> Mamma, young people are the future. I can no longer run, but I'd like to pass on the torch to them, like at the Olympics. They have only one life and it's worth spending it well.[114]

She devoted herself particularly to living and praying for those who did not have faith, in accordance with what Chiara Lubich asked her to do. She took that request to heart because she knew that without the gift of faith people do not have the happiness of knowing they are loved by God.[115] In November 1983, she wrote to Chiara:

> I realized I could find him [Jesus forsaken] in those who seem far from God, in atheists, and that I should love them in a very special way, without any ulterior motives![116]

In June 1984, at the conclusion of the international Gen 3 congress, she recorded a message for Chiara Lubich that included these words:

> I want to take the Ideal to all the people who are far from God. I know that will be more difficult at home, but saying this to you I commit myself, and I know I'll do it.[117]

A few days before her friend's death, Chicca jotted down something Chiara Luce said: *"I offer everything for the Assembly* and for those who are far from God."*[118]

It is significant that one of the most beautiful books about Chiara Luce was written by an agnostic who has continued a dialogue with her even after her death. This shows us that the Church, immersed in human realities, brings a seed of salvation, but also receives enrichment from them. Chiara Badano herself expresses this: *"Sometimes, they're better than we are."*[119]

Her secret of happiness, so evident in the two sentences cited in the introduction, lies in her hearing the Word of God and putting it into practice: *"Blessed rather are those who hear the word of God and obey it."*[†]

One word of God that Chiara Badano treasured above all others was the gospel verse that Chiara Lubich suggested to her as the reflection and summary of her life: *"Those who abide in me and I in them bear much fruit, because apart from me you can do nothing"* (Jn 15:5).

She focused her life intensely on the highest and best form of spreading the gospel, the new commandment of mutual love: *"By this everyone*

---

* The General Assembly of the Work of Mary gathers every six years.
† See Lk 11:28.

will know that you are my disciples, if you have love for one another" (Jn 13:35).

Another beatitude that characterized her life was faith in the resurrection, a faith that increased each time she embraced the Crucified-Risen Lord in her own suffering. Indeed, the gospel promises such happiness: *"Blessed is she who believed"* (Lk 1:45). In the final analysis, Chiara Luce transmits a message of happiness in faith. She wants us to be happy as she was: *"Be happy because I am."* And she has shown us the way.

Being rooted in the word of eternal life (Jn 6:28), she bore much fruit and reached the entire world, captivating thousands of young people with her style of holiness. She fulfilled what Chiara Lubich wished for the Gen 3, as well as for all young people: *"Aim further: at your country, at everyone's country, at the world."*[120]

I believe...world to come. Amen.

"Blessed are those who have not seen and yet have come to believe" (Jn 20:29). It could be said that Chiara Luce had a clear vision of the truth, as Augustine of Hippo promises to those who persevere in the faith: *"Now you are believers, and by persevering in the faith, you will become prophets*

*and know the truth."** Isn't that the real meaning of her name, Chiara Luce [clear light]—to
receive the light of truth? As a witness who
united herself to the suffering of Jesus, she
united herself to his resurrection and she saw in
the light the truths of our faith, as we have tried
to illustrate above. She also professed with her
life the other articles of the creed, which derive
as logical consequences from the resurrection.

I believe in the holy Catholic Church. Chiara
Luce's life was a period of gestation that prepared her for Life, enveloped in the holiness of
a Church that always needs to be purified.

She lived in an outstanding way the *communion of saints* in the Holy Spirit, within a
community/church where each person lives,
gives and receives, so that Christ in their
midst might live and work. She wrote to the
young people that they are on the front lines
in bringing the Ideal of unity: *"In my* stabat[†]
is your going."[121] With these words that seem
in contrast, she expressed the new logic into
which, like St. Paul, she had entered: *"So death
is at work in us, but life in you"* (2 Cor 4:12). This
is the communion of saints.

---

* *Homilies on the Gospel of John 1-40, Works of Saint
Augustine* (Hyde Park, NY: New City Press, 2009),
601.

† *Stabat*: a Latin word for "staying." See *Essential
Writings,* 140.

United to Jesus, who took upon himself the sins of the world, she offered her own sins as gifts and took on those of the others; she believed in *the forgiveness of sins.* She expressed her faith in the *resurrection of the body* when she accepted without shame the decline of her body, which she wanted clothed in a bridal gown. As a disciple of the One who has words of eternal life, she already possessed *the eternal life,* which consists in knowing the Father and Jesus Christ whom he has sent.[*] She experienced this same divine life when there was love circulating among all, and she told her mother not to spoil the surprise by telling her who would come out to meet her when she got to Heaven.

In the clear light of faith, she transmits to us her fervent testimony and her love, and she invites us to repeat with her: "Come Holy Spirit! Come Lord Jesus!"

---

[*] See Jn 17:3.

Abbreviations

Bible

Biblical references unless otherwise noted are taken from the New Revised Standard Version ©1989 Division of Christian Education of the National Council of Churches of Christ in the United States of America.

Church Documents

LG   Second Vatican Council Dogmatic Constitution on the Church, *Lumen Gentium,* 1964.

NMI John Paul II, Apostolic Letter, *Novo millennio ineunte,* 2001.

Written sources and reported words of Chiara Luce Badano. Original documents are in Italian, we provide our translation throughout.

Inf   *Informatio super virtutibus, in Congregatio Positio super vita, virtutibus et fama sanctitatis,* vol. 1, Roma 2004. [Information concerning her virtue, submitted to the Congregation for Determining Sainthood: from the position paper concerning her life, virtue and reputation for sainthood].

Summ *Summarium super virtutibus, in Congregatio De Causis Sanctorum, Beatificationis et Canonizationis Servae Dei Clarae Badano, Positio super vita, virtutibus et fama sancti- tatis,* vol. 1, Roma 2004. [Summary statement concerning virtue, Congregation for Determining Sainthood of the Servant of God Chiara Badano; from the position paper concerning her life, virtue and reputation for sainthood].

P2 *Biographia documentatain Congregation De Causis Sanctorum, Beatificationis et Canonizationis Servae Dei Clarae Badano, Positio super vita, virtutibus et fama sancti- tatis,* vol. 2, Roma 2004. [Biographical documents, Congregation for Determining Sainthood of the Servant of God Chiara Badano; from the position paper concerning her life, virtue and reputation for sainthood].

Unpub Unpublished letters sent by Chiara Luce and by Chicca Coriasco to the Gen 3 assistant of Genoa, Italy, which give precise details of their meetings.

Works by Chiara Lubich

WD *When did we see you Lord?* (Hyde Park, NY: New City Press, 1979)

G3 *To the Gen 3* (Rome: Città Nuova,1979)

EL *Early Letters, At the Origins of a New Spirituality* (Hyde Park, NY: New City Press, 2012)

UJF   *Jesus The Heart of His Message , Unity and Jesus Forsaken* (Hyde Park, NY: New City Press, 1985)

CR   *In cammino col Risorto* (Rome: Città Nuova,1987)

EW   *Essential Writings*, compiled by Michel Vandeleene (Hyde Park, NY: New City Press, 2007)

Endnotes

1. G3, 45.
2. P2, 115.
3. Summ, 83.
4. Inf, 51.
5. Inf, 107.
6. Summ, 56.
7. Pasquale Foresi, "Come pregare," Nuova Umanità (September/October 2005): 634. Our translation.
8. Summ, 156-57, 90.
9. Summ, 156-57.
10. Unpub.
11. Summ, 89-90.
12. P2, 189.
13. WD, 50 and 54.
14. P2, 115.
15. P2, 451.
16. P2, 415.
17. EL, 103.
18. Summ, 247.
19. Unpub.
20. Unpub.
21. Summ, 257.
22. P2, 356-57.
23. P2, 58.
24. Inf, 38.
25. Summ, 282.
26. *Letter 86 to Celine*, March 15, 1889.

27.   P2, 293.
28.   Summ, 160.
29.   CR, 159.
30.   P2, 166-67.
31.   Summ, 20.
32.   Summ, 268.
33.   Summ, 46.
34.   P2, 289.
35.   Summ, 293.
36.   EW, 87.
37.   Summ, 282.
38.   Unpub.
39.   Summ, 86.
40.   Summ, 279.
41.   P2, 119.
42.   Summ, 76.
43.   Summ, 101.
44.   Summ, 101.
45.   Summ, 281.
46.   P2, 129.
47.   EL, 90.
48.   Summ, 281.
49.   P2, 130.
50.   Summ, 281.
51.   P2, 215-216.
52.   P2, 354.
53.   EW, 94
54.   Summ, 35.
55.   Summ, 91.
56.   EW, 96.
57.   Inf, 107.
58.   P2, 292.
59.   Summ, 158.
60.   A testimony, Summ, 285.
61.   The Bishop of her diocese, Bishop Maritano, Summ, 49.
62.   Maria Teresa, her mother, one month before Chiara Luce's death, Summ, 75.

63.   Summ, 131.
64.   Summ, 39.
65.   Summ, 51.
66.   Summ, 39.
67.   P2, 288.
68.   Inf, 56.
69.   Inf, 107.
70.   Summ, 75.
71.   Inf, 107-08.
72.   Summ, 22.
73.   Summ, 75.
74.   P2, 354.
75.   P2, 291-92.
76.   Summ, 467.
77.   P2, 224.
78.   Summ, 94.
79.   Summ, 135.
80.   Summ, 54.
81.   Summ, 260.
82.   Summ, 48.
83.   EW, 95.
84.   P2, 291-92.
85.   Inf, 122.
86.   Summ, 292.
87.   Summ, 294.
88.   P2, 291.
89.   Summ, 161.
90.   Summ, 155.
91.   Summ, 154-55.
92.   Summ, 77.
93.   Summ, 49.
94.   NMI, 43.
95.   Summ, 261.
96.   Summ, 316.
97.   Summ, 346.
98.   Summ, 51. "Come Lord Jesus" is also known
       as the Maranatha Prayer which is Aramaic for

"Come Lord" as in 1 Corinthians 16:22 and Revelation 22:20.
99.   P2, 387.
100.   Summ, 154.
101.   Summ, 48.
102.   Summ, 46.
103.   Summ, 48.
104.   Collationes in Hexaemeron: 1, 4. (Our translation)
105.   EW, 135.
106.   P2, 514.
107.   Summ, 56.
108.   P2, 166-167.
109.   EW, 95.
110.   Summ, 21.
111.   Summ, 396.
112.   LG, 4.
113.   Summ, 400.
114.   P2, 362.
115.   P2, 189.
116.   P2, 130.
117.   Summ, 281.
118.   Summ, 56.
119.   Summ, 56.
120.   EW, 108.
121.   P2, 354.

Appendix

The Prayer to the Holy Spirit

*T*he prayer to the Holy Spirit* that Chiara Luce Badano recited.

Come Holy Spirit!

Come, Holy Spirit,
send forth the heavenly
radiance of your light.
Come, father of the poor,
come, giver of gifts,
come, light of the heart.
Greatest comforter,
sweet guest of the soul,
sweet consolation.
In labor, rest,
in heat, temperance,
in tears, solace.
O most blessed light,
fill the inmost heart

---

* *Veni Sancte Spiritus,* sometimes called the "Golden Sequence," is a sequence prescribed in the Roman Liturgy for the Masses of Pentecost.

of your faithful.
Without your grace,
there is nothing in us,
nothing that is not harmful.
Cleanse that which is unclean,
water that which is dry,
heal that which is wounded.
Bend that which is inflexible,
fire that which is chilled,
correct what goes astray.
Give to your faithful,
those who trust in you,
the sevenfold gifts.
Grant the reward of virtue,
grant the deliverance of salvation,
grant eternal joy.

Also available in the "15 Days of Prayer" series:

Blessed Frederic Ozanam, Christian Verheyde
    978-1-56548-487-0, paper
    978-1-56548-522-8, ebook
Brother Roger of Taize, Sabine Laplane
    978-1-56548-349-1, paper
    978-1-56548-375-0, ebook
Dietrich Bonhoeffer, Matthieu Arnold
    978-1-56548-344-6, ebook
Henri Nouwen, Robert Waldron
    978-1-56548-384-2, ebook
Jean-Claude Colin, François Drouilly
    978-1-56548-435-1, paper
Saint Augustine, Jaime Alvarez García
    978-1-56548-489-4, paper
    978-1-56548-535-8, ebook
Dorothy Day, Michael Boover
    978-1-56548-491-7, paper
    978-1-56548-567-9, ebook
Saint Benedict, André Gozier
    978-1-56548-304-0, paper
    978-1-56548-340-8, ebook

Saint Bernadette of Lourdes, François Vayne
    978-1-56548-343-9, ebook
Saint Catherine of Siena, Chantal van der Plancke
    and André Knockaert
    978-1-56548-342-2, ebook
Saint Clare of Assisi, Marie-France Becker
    978-1-56548-371-2, paper
    978-1-56548-405-4, ebook
Saint Faustina Kowalska, John J. Cleary
    978-1-56548-350-7, paper
    978-1-56548-499-3, ebook
Saint Francis of Assisi, Thaddée Matura
    978-1-56548-315-6, paper
    978-1-56548-341-5, ebook
Saint John of the Cross, Constant Tonnelier
    978-1-56548-427-6, paper
    978-1-56548-458-0, ebook
Saint Thérèse of Lisieux, Constant Tonnelier
    978-1-56548-391-0, paper
    978-1-56548-436-8, ebook
Saint Vincent de Paul, Jean-Pierre Renouard
    978-1-56548-357-6, paper
    978-1-56548-383-5, ebook
Thomas Merton, André Gozier
    978-1-56548-363-7, ebook

NEW CITY PRESS
of the Focolare
Hyde Park, New York
www.newcitypress.com

New City Press is one of more than 20 publishing houses sponsored by the Focolare, a movement founded by Chiara Lubich to help bring about the realization of Jesus' prayer: "That all may be one" (John 17:21). In view of that goal, New City Press publishes books and resources that enrich the lives of people and help all to strive toward the unity of the entire human family. We are a member of the Association of Catholic Publishers.

Also from New City Press

World of GeeBee & W (DVD); Walter Kostner
             978-1-56548-252-4 $5.95
> With lovable clown-like faces, these two pals discover some of life's most valuable lessons all in a days' play.

Gospel for Children; John J. Piantedosi & Ben Cioffi (Illustrator) 978-1-56548-370-5 $13.95
> Introduces preschool and middle-school-aged children to Jesus through the major events in his life.

Chiara Badano (DVD); Maria A. Calo
             978-1-56548-424-5 $15.95
> Filmed on location in Italy, this powerful film tells the story of Blessed Chiara Badano from her childhood to her beatification in 2010.

Chiara Luce: Life Lived to the Full; Michele Zanzucchi   978-1-56548-527-3 $9.95
> An inspiring biography as seen through her writings, her parents' eyes and her friends.

New Horizons; Chiara Amirante
             978-1-90503-910-4 $14.95
> It is a novel, a thriller and a love story, but above all it is a beacon of hope in our broken society.

Realizarse a los 18; Michele Zanzucchi
             978-9-50586-253-5 $13.50
> Vida y huella de Chiara "Luce" Badano.